Reverberations
of Dissent

Reverberations of Dissent

Identity and Expression in Iran's Illegal Music Scene

BRONWEN ROBERTSON

continuum

Continuum International Publishing Group

The Tower Building	80 Maiden Lane
11 York Road	New York
London	NY 10038
SE1 7NX	

www.continuumbooks.com

Library of Congress Cataloging-in-Publication Data
Robertson, Bronwen.
Reverberations of dissent : identity and expression in Iran's illegal music scene / Bronwen Robertson.
p. cm.
Includes bibliographical references and index.
ISBN-13: 978-1-4411-4649-6 (hardcover : alk. paper)
ISBN-10: 1-4411-4649-0 (hardcover : alk. paper)
ISBN-13: 978-1-4411-2325-1 (pbk. : alk. paper)
ISBN-10: 1-4411-2325-3 (pbk. : alk. paper)
1. Rock music--Iran--History and criticism. 2. Music--Political aspects--Iran. I. Title.

ML3534.6.I72R63 2012
781.660955--dc23

2012003059

ISBN: HB: 978-1-4411-4649-6
PB: 978-1-4411-2325-1

Typeset by Fakenham Prepress Solutions, Fakenham, Norfolk NR21 8NN
Printed and bound in the United States of America

CONTENTS

LIST OF FIGURES

INTRODUCTION

In Iran you need three things to be a proper band. First, you need band mates, then you need a practice space and then you need a Myspace page.[1]

(SIA, PERSONAL COMMUNICATION, OCTOBER 2007)

Figure 1 Tehran's suburbs on a typically smoggy day

Constituting a small minority of Tehran's vast population, Iran's unofficial rock musicians are, by and large, young men aged 17–30. They come from middle to upper-class families, live in the affluent northern suburbs of Tehran, are competent users of technology and are highly educated. Their socio-economic status is important because it is expensive to be an unofficial rock musician. There is no money to be made in a craft that is not officially recognized by an internal music industry and instruments and equipment are costly. Unofficial rock music is an elitist genre in Iran and in poorer communities Hip Hop is far more prevalent. While rappers need only their voice and a backing track, unofficial rock musicians need amps, cables, guitars, pedals and (usually) expensive musical training.

Although there are unofficial rock musicians in Iran's other metropo-
lises, an overwhelming majority of them are concentrated in Tehran.[2]
Their music has invariably been called 'underground' and 'alternative',
but in focus group interviews they pushed for a renaming of the scene,
at least in an academic and philosophical context, to 'unofficial' (Persian:
gheir-e rasmi) or 'illegal' (Persian: *gheir-e ghanooni*), claiming that these
descriptors are more accurate representations of their scene. While they
do still refer to their own music as 'underground' in casual conversation
with each other and in their promotional material, they find the term
contextually problematic. Houshang, guitarist and vocalist of the group
Aluminium MGS stated:

> The real meaning of underground is that you're going in the opposite
> direction of the current art movement; you're doing your own thing. But
> it's not like that in Iran . . . here it's a more literal underground. (Focus
> group interview, 9 July 2008)

While Tehran's unofficial rock musicians draw musical and stylistic influence
from bands and musicians outside Iran and are very aware of international
politics and trends, many have never travelled outside the country. Even
though they may have the financial capital to be able to do so, a lot of the
musicians I spoke with do not have passports, because either they have
not yet completed their compulsory military service or they refuse to do
so. They travel behind the Iranian government's pervasive internet filtering
to access social networking sites and watch the news and foreign entertainment programming on satellite television in order to access the outside
world. Due to both social (as a general rule, children stay in the family
home until marriage) and economic (the ever-increasing cost of living and
extraordinarily high unemployment rates) pressures, most of the musicians
I interviewed still lived with their parents. Their socialization has always
taken place behind closed doors, where they hold temporary autonomy and
have the freedom to be their true selves. Much of unofficial rock music's
significance can be found in this, its private and contested status in the
Islamic Republic of Iran.

Examining the unofficial rock music scene in Tehran as a participant/
observer for a year meant that research relationships quickly developed into
strong friendships. Together we endured the not-so-easy life of living in a
city overflowing with people: bad smells and worse driving. People hooked
up, fell out with each other, got together with their ex's best friend (just to
annoy them) and ate a lot of *ghorme sabzi*.[3] Everyone said that their mother
was the best cook in Iran, and I placated them all by agreeing. The youngest
of my interviewees was 17, the oldest 86, but most of them were university-
educated, unemployed, 20-something-year-olds who lived with their parents
and spent most of their time either working on creative projects, hanging

out with friends, or both. Most of the musicians that I interviewed were male and at the time I was working with Tehran's unofficial rock music scene I came across only one active female musician, a heavy rock vocalist.[4]

In Iran gender segregation is imposed across society from a very young age. While primary schools and high schools are single sex, most universities are co-educational. Social rules for young men and young women are very different and it is far more socially acceptable for a young woman to play classical music than it is for her to be in a rock band. Young Iranian women are very prevalent in the scene as photographers, poets, writers, graphic designers, and painters. Heavy rock singer Maryam said, 'Because I'm a girl it's hard to find people who want to come over and actually work on music without having a hidden [sexual] agenda . . . In the end it all comes down to traditional Iranian culture, ingrained patriarchy – the belief that only men can do certain things' (3 July 2008).

Those musicians who had formed bands practised most days of the week and the rest jammed at parties and recorded their music in home studios. I downloaded or was given samples of music by a wide range of musicians and some of these tracks are examined in the later chapters of this book. Whenever the opportunity arose I went to studios, practice rooms, concerts and gatherings, taking notes and photographs and asking questions. As a member of Tehran's unofficial rock music scene I attended social gatherings, concerts, chatted with other scene members online, hung out in studios, and lent my own musical talents as a violinist to various recordings. If it were not for the openness, sincerity and hospitality of my vivid Iranian friends, I could not have endeavoured to present their stories here, and to them I am eternally grateful. They patiently taught me their language, accepted my errors and overlooked my cultural faux pas. Theirs is a story about being driven to create: to create art, to create music, to create a world of their own completely separate from the strictly regulated order of their everyday lives.

How I first became interested in Iran's unofficial rock music scene is a story in itself. Media representations of Iran have constructed a skewed perspective of the country. Outside Iran most people have little idea about what goes on socially and culturally within this country's guarded borders. However, the fact that the Iranian government is strict in its censorship and control of state broadcasting media means that those living inside these borders are also misinformed. The principal intent of this book is to provide an account of a rapidly evolving music scene as it was experienced by the researcher through an extended period of participant-observation fieldwork and during ongoing research through and with the internet. Although the scene to be researched represents a very small proportion of the Iranian population, it provides a valuable insight into one of Iran's many secretive societies. Iranian homes are more than just living spaces. They are places of autonomy, beyond the rigorous reach of the state, where inhabitants and their acquaintances seek education and enjoy entertainment. Book clubs, parties, dance classes, yoga lessons and band practices all find sanctuary behind high fences, locked doors and video entry phones. This book will challenge some stereotypical misconceptions about Iran and it is hoped that those who read the following chapters will be inspired by the creativity and resilience of the members of Tehran's unofficial rock music scene.

This book is the product of my interaction with a very particular scene and this scene has shaped me as a person as much as my research and presence has affected it. While living in Tehran from July 2007 to July 2008 I became an active member in Tehran's unofficial rock music scene. My roles were multiple: enthusiast, participant, confidante, assistant and researcher. At first I navigated Tehran in a combination of broken Persian and English spoken slowly with a pseudo-American accent (the most comfortable accent for Iranians to understand due to their avid consumption of American film and music). But as the first semester of my Persian lessons came to a close I stood with confident poise on street corners ready to hail shared taxis, bargained for goods in the bazaars and expertly telephoned all manner of delivery services to feed and entertain a growing circle of friends within the comfort of my rented apartment.

Before venturing to Iran I had armed myself with the technology I would need to record practice sessions, interviews and, I hoped, concerts. Wanting to take a bare minimum of equipment so as not to draw unwanted attention to myself on the way in and out of Iran, a handheld digital video camera, a small digital camera, a laptop computer and a Sound Devices digital sound recorder with a stereo microphone became my arsenal. This, I thought, was about the limit before I started to look like a journalist or reporter. But I need not have worried because upon arrival at Tehran's Imam Khomeini Airport there were billboards advertising competitive broadband and laptop packages, small children were snapping away happily on state of the art digital SLR cameras and there were video cameras in the hands of religious clerics. There were basic but well-equipped recording studios in the homes of many of the musicians. It was, as the saying goes, 'like carrying coals to Newcastle'. There was, in fact, little need for any of the equipment I had, as the musicians had their own archives of the scene on the hard drives of their computers. On my intermittent visits to Paytakht, a multi-storey shopping complex specializing in electronics, I would always bump into a friend or acquaintance who was indulging in the same techno-luxuries as me. Importers working with Dubai and China were bringing in products at reasonable prices, skirting the strict economic sanctions by working with offshore agents of US companies like Hewlett-Packard. Paytakht is also a popular place to shop for software. One musician boasted that his cache of plug-ins for the cracked version of Cubase installed on his computer would have cost hundreds of thousands of dollars if he had purchased official versions.

This research on the unofficial rock music scene in Tehran is multi-sited. The members of the scene do not inhabit a single and static geographic location. Some were in Iran, some were in diaspora and some were on international tours. Some participate in the scene by buying CDs or downloading music, some perform concerts and audiences cram into any space when they do in order to take advantage of the rare occasion. The scene includes the spaces in which music is created and consumed and the people who inhabit those spaces. It encompasses the people that interact with the people who inhabit those spaces as well as the people who own or control those spaces. The unofficial rock music scene in Tehran comprises musicians, their support networks (friends, parents, fans), graphic artists, filmmakers, concertgoers and the impinging forces of censorship emanating from the Iranian government.

From the inception of my research I also inhabited multiple geographic spaces. First in New Zealand, where I met Manouchehr (discussed below), then Melbourne, Australia, where I spent a lot of time with the Iranian diasporic community, then Kensington, London, where I lived and inter-acted with London's large community of Iranians. I seemed to become a magnet for Iranians, meeting them in unexpected places: a hotel lobby in France, a New Zealand-bound aeroplane from London, the local hairdresser's and the sauna. Research opportunities were sought out but more often than not they blindsided me. It was after being accepted as a member of Tehran's unofficial rock music scene that I began to realize the impact of my existence in 'the field'. I organized parties and invited my friends, who belonged to different factions of the scene. They then met new people, formed alliances and instigated collaborations with each other that perhaps would not have eventuated without my intervention.

Prior to going to Iran I scoured scholarly literature and alternative media sources for opinions and theories about youth, music and life in Iran. I had been bombarded with media portrayals of Iran as a closed entity, a swathe of black-clad women and bearded men, an old, traditional country, anti-West and pro-nuke. But now I was reading about a dispro-portionately young population, a plastic surgery and party population, a Coca Cola-drinking Marlborough Light-smoking population. From the very outset it felt as if Iran were the epitome of a contradiction. I lived in Tehran for exactly 365 days, first in the suburb of Sayyed Khandan, in a small studio flat in the basement of an apartment building, then in a villa in Farmaniyeh with a Danish student and an Iranian UNESCO worker, and finally in a sprawling pre-revolutionary mansion, which was as decrepit as the two octogenarian women with whom I shared it. Tehran is a tense and polluted city, but I quickly found myself surrounded by a few hundred incredibly creative youth. I conducted intensive, multi-sited, participant-observation research and was fortunate to have a relatively unique status as a young foreign musician/researcher.

Anthropologists Gupta and Ferguson ask for a serious reconsideration of the boundaries of the 'field' (1997: 5), and argue that it is only by decentralizing the field that we can move into a 'mode of study that cares about, and pays attention to, the interlocking of multiple social-political sites and locations' (37). This type of multi-sited 'field' research invokes a particular set of issues concerning ethnographic representation. In order to deal with the complex interplay of dialectics that came from researching in so many different spaces and times in a logical manner I turned to the writing of Marcus, who argues for the need to discuss the interdependence among multiple research locales (1986: 171). My research locales were both physical and virtual, some took place at a particular moment in time and some evolved over extended periods. In the narratives that are interwoven throughout this book I hope to represent fairly the intricacy and uniqueness of the lives of Tehran's young unofficial rock musicians. With pre-emptive apologies for the narcissistic yet necessary digression that follows, permit me to start at the approximate beginning, because my own interests have very much shaped my approach to research.

Educated classically in music from a very young age, I was never very interested in its conventions. My first real taste of rebellion occurred when I founded a rock band with a high school friend. We were 14 and the heaving bass lines and distorted guitars thrilled us. Crafting catchy lyrics to shout over repetitive chord sequences and playing at intense speeds and volumes became a passion; the instant gratification of rock music certainly satiated. This medium proved to be an easy way to communicate with our peers using music; they had demonstrated little interest in the classical music that we had previously performed. Playing in a rock band upped my social standing and came packaged with much-needed kudos. This early exposure to rock music performance fuelled my interest in the audience as a reactive membership group and it was around this time that I started investigating how audiences react to music, how a message can be conveyed through music, and how musical conventions can be subverted through music itself. This book is, in part, about conventions, control, subversion and interaction.

Growing up in a small island nation at the 'bottom' of the world (New Zealand) meant relative cultural isolation for many of my generational peers, but I experienced the sights and sounds of other countries through both physical and virtual travel. Accompanying my academic mother on frequent overseas excursions allowed me opportunities that few of my school and university friends could even envisage. Another peculiarity of my childhood was my very early exposure to the internet.[5] In 1992, my mother and I corresponded with each other from antipodal points on the globe using a 14.4 Kb/s dialup modem and a Macintosh Classic computer with a black and white screen. I was 8 years old and she was on sabbatical in the US. My grandparents, accustomed to their handwritten letters taking weeks to cross the world, were overwhelmed by the technology, so I printed out mum's emails for them to read and transcribed their replies. And, as I gaze into the millions of colours beaming from the matte screen of this MacBook Pro, connected wirelessly to a router transmitting a 10 Mb/s broadband connection, I marvel at how technologies, and the ways that they are used, have changed dramatically over a relatively short period of time. During my childhood and teenage years I overcame my geographic isolation by communicating and interacting electronically with a burgeoning global youth culture via the internet. Isolation is a commonality that links New Zealand and Iran; New Zealand is geographically isolated, Iran politically so. During the preliminary research phase, initial contacts were made using global communications technologies and I continue to maintain strong ties with Iran through the same means. This book is partly about how technology has evolved and permeated our everyday lives, allowing many of us to cross geo-political borders and circumvent state control with a series of clicks.

My first year at university in 2001 coincided with the most widely broadcast and historically traumatic event to hit the western consciousness in my lifetime – 9/11. Following the attack on New York's 'Twin Towers', negative portraits of Middle Eastern countries and their governments again dominated the evening news programmes of the western world. New Zealand's news media was no exception and this was the first time many people my age were exposed to any imagery from contemporary Iran, as it was absent from our history books and social studies manuals. We saw pictures of Iranians swathed in black and waving multi-coloured, mass-produced placards chanting 'Death to America' in their streets and we thought, and were led to believe, that this was the real face of Iran. Despite New Zealand's very diverse cultural and ethnic makeup I had yet to meet an Iranian . . . and then I met Manouchehr.[6]

Manouchehr worked in a small, bustling café near where I worked. Despite acquiring New Zealand citizenship, Manouchehr's environmental engineering degree, which was gained from an Iranian academic institution, was not recognized. Unable to work in his academic field, he skilfully assembled more than 100,000 delicious kebabs a year. The eight years it took for Manouchehr to work his way from Iran to New Zealand, stowing away on ships and using a fake Greek passport to clear customs as he went, had carved deep lines into his face, which his ever-present smile exaggerated. This smile provided a mask for his traumatic history. Manouchehr fled Iran during the Iran–Iraq War (1980–1988) after one of his brothers died in combat. From the war stories he shared, it became clear that his ingenuity had saved his own life on many occasions. A military mechanic, Manouchehr was emotionally attached to a decrepit green BMW that he had saved from the brink of extinction several times. He ritualistically dissected and reconstructed it when it broke down, which seemed to satiate a do-it-yourself desire that I also observed in the unofficial musicians with whom I became acquainted in Iran. Another theme threaded throughout this book is Iranian ingenuity, which prevails during the most testing of times.

One cold autumn day in the early months of 2002, in the passenger seat of Manouchehr's sea green BMW, my life changed. It was raining relentlessly and I stowed my bicycle in the trunk, accepting Manouchehr's generous offer of a ride home. As the BMW jolted to life, a mesmerizing female voice filled the tinny speakers. It was obvious from the hiss of the chewed cassette that it had been listened to hundreds of times. Manouchehr hastily ejected the cassette, switched on a banal easy listening radio station, and turned up the volume. Assuming I would prefer to listen to the radio, he was surprised when I urged him to play the cassette again. Smiling, he informed me that this lush contralto belonged to Googoosh, and that the recording was made before the Iranian Revolution (1979). Manouchehr translated the lyrics to '*Gol bi Goldoon*' (lit. 'flower without a vase') for me in a singsong voice:

> One cold autumn day you broke free of your vase; you sat waiting in the greenhouse like the bride of flowers. Spring will come, and I'll bring you again, to plant you in the greenhouse, oh beautiful flower. Once more, you'll tell your vase, 'stay with me forever'. You say, 'without you I'll die, there can be no flower without a vase' . . . What a mistake I made, I believed what you said . . . But she'll make the same mistake as me, she'll believe what you say.

The heavily laden metaphors piqued my curiosity; the Persian, comprising sounds my mouth was unaccustomed to uttering, and naturally falling into a lilted six-beat rhythm, was beautiful.[7] The most affecting aspect for me was the dissimilarity between the Iranians I was being introduced to and the ones who were being depicted on television. In stark contrast to the macabre images broadcast by the media, these Iranians danced, laughed and sang, and I wanted to know more. This book is also about stereotypes, contradictions and historical and political contexts.

In 2005, when I began researching Googoosh and the pre-revolutionary popular music scene for my Honours thesis at the University of Melbourne (see Robertson 2005), I had yet to hear any unofficial rock music. The young Iranians I befriended through conducting participant-observation field research in Melbourne's Iranian community listened mainly to post-revolutionary pop music made in diaspora. They also listened to pre-revolutionary pop music and Googoosh's popularity proved unfaltering. After discovering how pre-revolutionary popular music and music produced in diaspora were illegally distributed through Iran's black market, I assumed that there must also be types of illegal music being produced within Iran's borders. It was through using Myspace to promote my own music that I unearthed a small but very well established niche of unofficial Iranian rock bands. These bands were using the same technologies to produce and distribute their music as the network of musicians surrounding me in Melbourne and they immediately commanded my attention.

Like us, they were producing music in their bedrooms using basic recording equipment and distributing the final product via the internet. From that point on my research was dedicated to finding out exactly how, where and why unofficial Iranian rock bands perform, produce, distribute and consume music. Very early in the research process it became obvious that a trip to Iran to conduct participant-observation fieldwork was imperative. Although the music being produced illegally in Iran was easy to access using the internet technology available to me in Melbourne, the context of its production and consumption was invisible. I needed to see and experience its production and distribution first hand. This book is about how these secret sounds are disseminated and, as they reverberate, how they affect both Iranian and global youth culture.

This brief autobiography contextualizes this research in terms of the researcher; my close connection to both the research topic and those whom I interviewed has left me feeling heavy under the weight of implication. Taking part in the scene as a participant and a researcher has had both benefits and disadvantages. It was not always easy to distance myself from the research topic and at times I found that my judgement became clouded by my emotional attachment. As I write I can hear the voices and see the faces of all those whose personal experiences are narrated in this book. First and foremost, they are my friends. My own allegiances have been explicated in this introduction in order to avoid criticism for being too tangled up in the research at a later date. Farhang Rouhani's (2004: 685–6) definition of the 'field' resonates strongly with me: '[The 'field' comprises] multiple spaces, times, and priorities [which are] constituted through the activities of the researcher in those spaces and times'.

I found myself to be constantly 'in the field', no matter where I was geographically situated; there was no 'off' button, not programmed into this researcher at least. This book is as much about transcending boundaries as it is about being restricted by them.

Together we will explore how a select group of Tehrani youth creates and expresses divergent identities in a politically and socially subversive way by writing and performing unofficial rock music in the Islamic Republic of Iran. As these musicians promote and distribute their work among themselves and to others outside the scene they are forging their own community while simultaneously contributing to global youth culture.[8]

The unofficial rock music scene has evolved rapidly during the first decade of the twenty-first century and the diversity of this scene needs to be captured. By discussing a side of Iran seldom represented in the foreign media I hope to initiate new ways of thinking about how young people fight for reform when repressed and how they desire to create, even while their everyday lives are subject to state scrutiny and control. Despite the Iranian government's ongoing efforts to restrict media consumption and censor literature and the arts, the Iranian youth discussed in this book continue to use these media to subvert that power.

This book asks the questions: what motivates people to play music without permission? What type of people produce and perform illegal music and why? What are the consequences or rewards of performing and producing illegal music? How does Iran's unofficial rock music disseminate and affirm unique, alternative and oppositionist identities? Is it possible that these identities, especially when perpetuated collectively, can have a reaffirming effect on those who grew up in the isolating first years of the Islamic Republic of Iran? Can these oppositional identities eventually bring about social and political change? And, what hope is there for their futures?

Members of Tehran's unofficial rock music scene find their voices, deal with their struggles, and shape their identities by performing, recording, promoting and consuming unofficial rock music. The sense of community and feeling of togetherness that playing music can create is particularly poignant in Iran, where the current ultra-conservative regime's weather-beaten umbrella is struggling to hold its shape in the face of ever stronger gusts of ingenuity and creativity from beneath. How is music utilized to present, represent and affirm the self in a society where social class and religiosity have, for centuries, defined a series of conventional and widely accepted social roles? The weight of censorship and social and governmental rules has instilled in Iran's unofficial rock musicians a deep-seated desire to produce and consume illegal music in spite of, or perhaps because of, the consequences.

Notes

1   Due to the contested nature of the music being researched, pseudonyms have been used to protect the identities of the interviewees in cases where direct quotes have been presented.

2   One such band is *Sad Sal-e Akhar* (lit. 'the past one hundred years') who hail from Mashhad. Their debut single '*Bar Ax*' (lit. 'opposite') can be streamed from their Facebook profile which is available at https://www.facebook.com/pages/Sad-Sale-Akhar-/176975075646033

3   *Ghorme sabzi*, a dish of stewed lamb, kidney beans, herbs and dried limes, is a staple dish from the varied and expansive Iranian cuisine.

4   Women musicians in Tehran's unofficial rock music scene are usually vocalists, but this is not a phenomenon unique to Iran. Famous women musicians

like P. J. Harvey, Shirley Manson (of the band Garbage) and Beth Gibbons (Portishead) are the front-women for all-male bands. Until the establishment of the Riot Grrrl movement of the early 1990s, which was influenced by Bikini Kill and Sleater Kinney, rock music was a male-dominated environment and, to some extent, it still is.

5 The word internet has been de-capitalized in this book in order to redefine it as both a changing environment and a tool for communication rather than the static place that is insinuated through its capitalization as a proper noun (for further discussion see Zorn 2009).

6 New Zealand is one of nine countries that host the most resettled refugees under the UN High Commissioner for Refugees' (UNHCR) Quota Programme.

7 The native word for the Persian language is Farsi, which is the Arabized form of Parsi. At the recommendation of my Iranian friends and an article by Kamran Talatoff (1997), a professor of Persian and Iranian studies, I have chosen to use the word Persian instead of Farsi in this book.

8 The term 'youth' is used in this book in a non-academic non-conceptual way, to refer broadly to those aged 16 to 30. The generation gap seems larger in Iran than it does elsewhere, and this is due in part to the socio-political context in which today's Iranian youth have come of age. They were born after the Iranian Revolution (1979) and grew up during the Iran–Iraq war (1980–1988). These two events have dramatically influenced their lives. The terms *javan* (lit. 'youth') and *now-javan* (lit. 'teenager') are used as broadly in Iran as their English counterparts are in the West. However, as is the case in the West, there are many different types of 'youth' and this book is about a very select group.

CHAPTER ONE

A political overview: from king to clergy

Tehran's unofficial rock music scene has evolved under a complex, convoluted and very unique set of political and social circumstances. In order to understand why this music is so controversial in the Islamic Republic of Iran, and to understand its growing significance as a tool for circumvention, we must look briefly back to pre-revolutionary Iran and examine the complex history of Iran as experienced by the grandparents and parents of contemporary youth for historical context. The policies of the Islamic Republic are deeply rooted in and drawn out from a complex and conservative society. In many cases, the policies enforced by the Islamic state are not so far removed from those imposed by the monarchy before the revolution and some see the Islamic regime to be almost a mirror image of the pre-revolutionary monarchy, its asymmetrical opposite. 1979's Iranian Revolution brought with it a shift in power from king to clergy and as Arjomand so eloquently argues, this was merely the substitution of 'the turban for the crown' (1988).

During the 1950s, pop and early rock music was supported and promoted by the monarchic regime of the Pahlavi dynasty (1925–1979). Iran's classical and folk musics waned in popularity during this period as the Shah's unwavering commitment to modernization began to seem like a veiled form of westernization. Iranians became increasingly frustrated with the Shah's dictatorial rule and they believed that his modernization agenda was degrading Iran's own culture and history.

When the Islamic government seized power in the aftermath of the 1979 Iranian Revolution, they set about eradicating all traces of the monarchy by changing street names and banning anything they thought was anti-Islam or had been tainted by the Shah's attempts at modernization/westernization. Despite their best efforts, these things did not disappear. To this day, 30 years on, some Iranians call Tehran's Vali Asr Street by its pre-revolutionary name (Pahlavi Avenue). The younger generation who call this street by its pre-revolutionary name are not doing so out of habit; they are too young to remember the monarchy and are doing so as a symbol of their resistance to the authorities. As will become apparent, cultural and social life merely retreated behind closed doors into the relative safety of the private home after the revolution and it is here where opportunities for subversion are most prevalent. This chapter provides a brief overview of the downfall of the monarchy and the instigation of the Islamic Republic, revealing how these two events have significantly impinged upon the lives of a baby boom generation of post-revolutionary Iranian youth.

Like father, like son? The Pahlavi dynasty and its downfall

In 1921, a soldier named Reza Khan had forced the Iranian government of the time to relinquish their authority with the help of the Russian-trained Cossack Brigade that he commanded. Four years later, although he was employed as an officer in their army, Reza Khan seized power from the collapsing Qajar dynasty and established the Pahlavi dynasty (see Ghani 2000). Reza Khan's coronation took place in 1926, and as he passed his first law, requiring all Iranians to have a surname, he renamed himself Reza Shah Pahlavi. Iranians did not have official surnames before this law was passed. They were known by their relationships to other places or people, by their occupation, or by where they were from. For example, 'Ali's son Arash', 'Reza the carpet weaver', or 'Mohammad from Shiraz'. Many chose names that reflected these elements becoming, for example, Arash Alizadeh, Reza Ghalibaf and Mohammad Shirazi. Reza Shah chose Pahlavi for his family because of its connection to pre-Islamic Iranian history. It is the name of the script that was used to write Persian before the Muslim conquest (633–644) forcibly introduced the Arabic script, and replaced the ancient Zoroastrian religion with Islam.

The introduction of the Uniformity of Dress Law in 1928 was a continuation of Reza Shah's attempts to push towards modernization and away from Islam (Hiro 1987: 26, Cronin 2003: 262–3). Reza Shah banned women from wearing the chador in public and introduced a western-style dress code, which included neckties, button-down shirts tucked in to trousers and a round peaked cap for men, which was nicknamed the Pahlavi cap. The prohibition of the chador forced many pious Iranian women to withdraw from the public sphere, as to go outdoors without their Islamic covering would tarnish the esteem of their families. The new law also affected Muslim men, who traditionally wear plain-coloured loose-hanging shirts with no collars.[1] Reza Shah's rules typically had negative effects on religious, poor and rural Iranians. In addition to these dress codes and the tax increases described below, he also reduced the number of students at theology schools and tightened restrictions on them by appointing standardized examination boards (Hiro 1987: 26).

For the second six months of my year in Tehran, I resided with octogenarian royalist Mahsa in leafy Darband, one of the city's northernmost suburbs. According to her, Reza Shah's (r. 1925–1941) biggest achievement was the development, during the 1930s, of a rail network that connected Tehran with the Persian Gulf in the very south of Iran and the Caspian Sea in the north. Mahsa took great pleasure in saying that Reza Shah accomplished this by increasing the tax on the price of sugar by 1 per cent. To Mahsa, this seemed ingenious, but to many Iranians the price increase was crippling. Iran's tribal populations were among the first to become displeased by the monarchy's ever-increasing taxes, as they were accustomed to trading rather than purchasing (Cronin 2003: 260–4).

In 1941, during World War II, British and Soviet forces invaded Iran. They labelled their invasion 'Operation Countenance' and during this time they forced the abdication of Reza Shah (Keith 2004: 226). The purpose of this invasion was to secure the financially lucrative Iranian oilfields and to ensure that their supply lines would be available to the Soviets as they fought against Germany. During this coup d'état the Soviets and the British placed Mohammad Reza Pahlavi (1919–1980), aged 21, onto his father's throne. They hoped that the prince would be more open to western political influence and this indeed proved to be the case. 'Operation Countenance' was neither the first nor the last time that foreign interference impinged upon Iranian politics and Dreyfuss (2005) argues that the US, through their interference with Iranian politics, has contributed to the rise of fundamentalist Islam and anti-western sentiment in Iran.[2]

In a much belated coronation ceremony in 1967 Mohammad Reza Shah Pahlavi crowned himself Shahan Shah (lit. 'king of kings'), Aryamehr (lit. 'light of the Aryans'), and Bozorg Arteshtaran (lit. 'head of the warriors'). In 1971 he may have jinxed himself by sponsoring a controversially opulent party for world leaders and royalty at the ancient ruins of Persepolis to celebrate 2500 years of unbroken Iranian monarchy (see Ansari 2003: 171; and Kadivar 2002). Khomeini, in his speeches, referred to this party as the 'Devil's Festival'. A chartered jet flew 159 chefs, bakers and waiters from Paris to Iran ten days before the event in preparation for serving more than five hundred guests who were all housed in luxury, purpose-built self-contained 'tents' (see Figure 2). Students in Qom protested against the Persepolis celebrations by highlighting the divide between the display of wealth on the one hand and the suffering famine stricken Fars and Baluchistan-Sistan provinces on the other (Hiro 1987: 56). The menu, which was leaked ahead of time, included roasted peacock and boiled quail eggs stuffed with Iranian caviar from the Caspian Sea. Defending his lavish spending the Shah reputedly said, 'What did they expect the Imperial Court of Iran to offer their guests, bread and radishes?' (in Kadivar 2002). This was a backhanded comment, as an Iranian dinner table would not be complete without *naan* (bread) and *sabzi* (a mixed combination of spicy salad leaves and radishes).

Figure 2 Forty years later, the skeletons of tents used for the 1971 Persepolis celebrations stand strong (photograph by Stina Bäcker, used with permission)

Mohammad Reza Pahlavi overturned many of his father's rulings while he was king, particularly those concerning Islam and the power of the clergy. In fact, he made it mandatory for governmental institutions to observe the Islamic prohibitions during Ramadan. Mohammad Reza Pahlavi also overturned the ban his father had placed on the performance of Islamic passion plays (Persian: *ta'aziyeh*), allowing them to take place during the month of Muharram, the first month of the Islamic calendar, a sacred month of remembrance for Imam Hussein, the prophet Mohammad's grandson. Mohammad Reza Pahlavi also increased the quota his father had implemented to limit the number of Iranians who were permitted to make the pilgrimage to Mecca per year.

Although Reza Shah's dress code remained intact, many urban women began appearing in public with the headscarf on and the police showed little interest in reprimanding them (see Hiro 1987: 30). Mohammad Reza Pahlavi relied heavily on his secret police SAVAK (Persian: *Sazeman-e Ettela'at va Amniyat-e Keshvar*, lit. 'National Intelligence and Security Organization') to impose order with physical force as political unrest compounded (see Afkhami 2009). SAVAK, a 60,000-strong armed force working in tandem with the Iranian Intelligence Ministry, received training in interrogation and torture methods from the CIA (McCoy 2006: 74).[3]

On a social level the inequity demonstrated by events such as the Persepolis celebration, the suppression of oppositionist thought, and the dictatorial control of the media caused widespread discontent throughout Iran and this discontent marked the beginning of the monarchy's eventual downfall. Many anti-monarchist groups participated fervently in the lead-up to the revolution including: *Hezb-e Tudeh-ye Iran* (the Marxist Tudeh Party, Party of the Masses), *Nahzat-e Azadi-ye Iran* (the Islamic Freedom Movement of Iran), and a revived version of the National Front. These parties are still active and have an online presence, although they are based in exile. The National Front, supported by the urban middle class, did not want to replace the Shah with a theocratic regime; they were simply pushing for the monarchy to adhere to the reforms that had been written into the 1906 constitution (Bashiriyeh 1984: 126, Jahanbakhsh 2001: 201; Hiro 1987: 103).

The Islamic Freedom Movement of Iran and the Marxist Tudeh Party did call for the Shah to be overthrown, but neither party anticipated a theocratic dictatorship. The Islamic Freedom Movement of Iran was included in the first parliament of the Islamic Republic of Iran but angered quickly when Khomeini neglected to use the word 'democratic' in the country's new name or anywhere in its new constitution. The Freedom Movement stormed out of parliament after Khomeini publicly endorsed the taking of hostages at the US Embassy building in Tehran. In spite of a large number of political parties being involved in the Shah's downfall, Ayatollah Khomeini emerged, by force, as the leader of Iran at the crux of the revolution.[4] From exile, through cassette tapes of his sermons that were smuggled across Iran's borders, reproduced, and mass distributed on the black market, Khomeini encouraged Iranians, who had already been mobilized through the work of other anti-monarchist groups, to strip away power from the monarchy.[5]

At a dinner party at Tehran's Niyavaran Palace on New Year's Eve in 1978, US President Carter proposed a toast to Mohammad Reza Pahlavi (r. 1941–1979), declaring Iran, under the leadership of the young king, to be '[An] island of stability in the troubled Middle East' (Anderson 2006: 115). Carter was hoping to rally support for the flailing king as Iran disintegrated into dissent but protests broke out in Qom a few weeks after Carter's visit. Religious scholars and students, harbouring a growing resentment towards the monarchy since the expulsion of their beloved Khomeini from Iran in 1964, decreed that the Pahlavi regime was un-Islamic. While this may indeed have been true, the government of the Islamic Republic of Iran are now emulating the domineering stronghold that the Pahlavi kings maintained over Iran for more than half a century through oppression, censorship and exorbitant military expenditure.

The new constitution, contradictions and conflicts of interest

The Iranian monarchy collapsed on 13 February 1979 and an overwhelming 98.2 per cent of voters said 'yes' in a referendum held on 31 March that gave the Iranian people two choices: did they want their country to become an Islamic Republic or not (see Arjomand 1988: 137; Bashiriyeh 1984: 155–7; Paidar 1995: 226–8). Moderate parties such as the National Democratic Front and most other regional parties boycotted the referendum but, according to official figures, there was a 79 per cent voter turnout (Hiro 1987: 438; Bashiriyeh 1984: 156). Although the Iranian people were against dictatorship and corruption, and many had been pushing for a democratic system of government, the word 'democratic' was not to be used anywhere in the country's new name of constitution because Khomeini decreed that it would belittle Islam, which is meant to be inherently democratic and just for all (Arjomand 1988: 137). Dr Cyrus Yeganeh, a sociology professor at Tehran's Art University, urged me to read the Constitution of the Islamic Republic of Iran (Persian: *Ghanoon-e Assasi-ye Jomhuri-ye Iran*) and to use it in my research. He argued that upon inspection I would find that the Iranian government does not act outside its constitutional rights.

A draft version of the constitution was modelled on the 1958 constitution of the French Fifth Republic (see Arjomand 2000). This was somewhat ironic considering that the clergy wanted to steer clear of western influence and ideals. However, the Assembly of Experts (the panel that monitors the efficacy of the Supreme Leader and has the power to impeach him) edited the document beyond recognition, and only the offices of President and Prime Minister remained borrowed from the French model.[6] One of the most controversial points of the new constitution was Article 107, which ascribed full control over Iran to a suitably qualified religious leader who would be called the Supreme Leader. The heroically pious Khomeini, who would act on behalf of God in the absence of Imam Zaman, the twelfth and final Imam, the ultimate redeemer of humankind, was to be Iran's first Supreme Leader (Arjomand 1988: 139). As yet there have only been two Supreme Leaders of the Islamic Republic of Iran. Khomeini was succeeded by Khamenei who, Melman and Javedanfar argue, was chosen because he had no outstanding allegations of corruption as some of the other candidates did (2008: 147). Khamenei was not an ayatollah at that time, though the title of ayatollah was bestowed upon him very shortly (and very conveniently) after Khomeini's death in 1989 (Sciolino 2001: 416).

The Constitution of the Islamic Republic of Iran looks relatively fair and just at first glance. The political system of the Islamic Republic should, according to the constitution, be based on '[the] negation of all forms of oppression, both the infliction of and the submission to it, and of dominance, both its imposition and its acceptance' (Article 2 [Foundation Principles], Chapter 1 General Principles, the Constitution of the Islamic Republic of Iran). The stated goals are, '[To ensure] the participation of the entire people in determining their political, economic, social, and cultural destiny . . . the abolition of all forms of *undesirable discrimination* and the provision of equitable opportunities for all' (Article 3 [State Goals], Chapter I, emphasis mine). Alarm bells start ringing. Why does a constitution need to distinguish between undesirable discrimination and ordinary discrimination?

In addition, the constitution clearly states, 'Public gatherings and marches may be freely held, provided arms are not carried' (Article 27 [Freedom of Assembly], Chapter III). But on 12 June 2008 I went to Mellat Park on Vali Asr Street to see if a protest that I had been hearing murmurs about in Tehran's public buses and taxis would actually take place. Protesters in the peaceful demonstration had hoped to make a stand against rising inflation and call for the release of Abbas Palizdar.[7] I arrived to see a group of official-looking men without uniforms chasing modestly dressed women away from the park's entrance, kicking them and threatening them with their batons.[8] There were hundreds of policemen on motorbikes doubling soldiers wielding AK-47s, but none of the protesters carried arms; they were simply carrying out their constitutional right. The soldiers and police took up strategic positions around the park. Police vans with tinted windows had cordoned off all of the main intersections. Soldiers with riot gear, helmets, shields and tasers were sweeping the street clear of demonstrators. The streets reeked of tear gas.

To reiterate, the constitution clearly states, 'Public gatherings and marches may be freely held, provided arms are not carried.' There is, however, a subclause that follows this article in the constitution. It continues, ' . . . [provided] that they [public gatherings and marches] are not detrimental to the fundamental principles of Islam' (Article 27 [Freedom of Assembly], Chapter III). The constitution itself never sets forth what the fundamental principles of Islam are and it seems that the principles of Islam that are fundamental for many pious Iranian people differ remarkably from those deemed fundamental by the Iranian authorities. This sentence acts as an escape clause. Other places this escape clause is used in the constitution include: 'Publications and the press have freedom of expression except when it is detrimental to the fundamental principles of Islam or the rights of the public' (Article 24 [Freedom of the Press]. Chapter III) and, 'The freedom of expression and dissemination of thoughts in the Radio and Television of the Islamic Republic of Iran must be guaranteed in keeping with the Islamic criteria and the best interests of the country' (Article 175 [Freedom of Expression, Government Control], Chapter XII).

The new Islamic government was intended to be a fair and just system. It was supposed to eliminate dictatorial rule and oppression, but the clever wording of the constitution has allowed for power-hungry individuals to work the system to their best advantage at the cost of Iran, which now has a Supreme

Leader in place of a King. Although Section Six of Article 3 of the constitution makes it clear that 'all forms of despotism and autocracy and all attempts to monopolize power' will be eliminated, the Supreme Leader chooses the head of the judiciary, six members of the Guardian Council (Persian: *Shora-ye Negahban-e Ghanoon-e Assasi*), the commanders of all of the armed forces and the head of *Seda o Sima*, Iran's national radio and television broadcasting organization. The judiciary (the head of which is chose by the Supreme Leader) nominates the six other members of the Guardian Council.

Iran's political system is an autocratic hierocracy controlled by the Supreme Leader. The constitution of the Islamic Republic can be likened to the children's string game 'cat's cradle'. The Iranian government, as defined by the constitution, comprises a tangled system of knots, mainly controlled by a second player, the Supreme Leader, reaching in from above. The complexity of the system is to disguise the fact that one person is in control, which would be against the constitution.

Constitutional politics have directly affected social and cultural life in Iran today. Although the constitution of the Islamic Republic has only been amended once since it was written, in 1989 when the office of Prime Minister and the need for the Supreme Leader to be a Grand Ayatollah were removed, society has changed dramatically. The next section of this chapter will focus on the ways that Iranian people have reacted against the harsh rules and regulations of the Islamic Republic of Iran and carved out some semblance of social reform for themselves.

Repression and resistance: 30 years of two steps forward and one shove back

DeBano advises us not to underestimate the power and pervasiveness of the Iranian authorities: 'There are a multitude of ways in which citizens are made aware that they are under the watchful, if not omniscient, eyes (and ears) of the nation' (2005: 442). Citizens are reminded of the watchfulness of the state by a special branch of the police force called *Gasht-e Ershad* (lit. 'Guidance Patrol'). *Gasht-e Ershad* has the most chic of all police uniforms – dark green starched straight outfits, tailored to fit and trimmed with black. The force's female contingent sport chadors and frowns and do not, under any circumstances, wear makeup. While on patrol *Gasht-e Ershad* stand in strict file, congregating around an equally ominous-looking van, checking passers-by for infringements in dress or behaviour.

Dress code violations are *Gasht-e Ershad's* main target and both men and women are affected. Any hairstyle, outfit or behaviour deemed to be offensive or illegal can result in an arrest. *Gasht-e Ershad's* presence is calculated and they are there to incite fear in those who must pass by.

They park their vans at main intersections, which makes them very visible; luckily, this also ensures that they are relatively easy to avoid. Although they enforce a strict code, the main reason they are there is to be seen and to have their presence felt. *Gasht-e Ershad* assume their positions just before rush hour and are scarcely seen at other times. On the city's busy Thursday nights, the last of the working week, *Gasht-e Ershad* are often positioned outside popular shopping malls, entertainment complexes and parks. Their purpose is to ensure that the populace feel surveilled, and their method is effective.

Figure 3 One of Tehran's ubiquitous propaganda portraits, painted on the side of an office building near to the former US Embassy in Tehran (photo by BT, used with permission)

Iranians are reminded of the state's stronghold over their public lives in a myriad of other ways. The scores of painted murals lining Tehran's autobahns and main streets are mostly austere images, faded portraits of war martyrs and revolutionary leaders like Khomeini, grim reminders of the loss of hundreds of thousands of lives during the Iran–Iraq war (1980–1988) and of Iran's fervent sponsorship of other Middle Eastern militant organizations such as the Hezbollah in Lebanon and Hamas in Palestine. But Tehran municipality's Urban Beautification Organization is trying to change this.

A subsection of the organization has been dedicated solely to the upkeep and commissioning of urban graphics and murals.[9] They still commission special commemorative portraits of important martyrs and maintain crucial propaganda images, such as the bleak murals adorning the buildings surrounding the former US Embassy (see Figure 3), but the organization is now endeavouring to cover Tehran's dusty landscape with bright, peaceful images (see Figure 4). Mohammad Reza Sharif Kazemi, the organization's spokesperson, argues that the old murals, while still significant and symbolic, no longer reflect contemporary times or resonate with the city's inhabitants. He believes the new murals depict universally understood themes, and hold significance for those who are too young to remember the events depicted on the city's walls. Mr Kazemi argues, 'Our approach is to have murals that are comforting, that ease the daily pressures of life on the people of Tehran . . . When we approve an idea, we consider the area's culture and history and try to strike a balance between modernism and traditionalism'.[10]

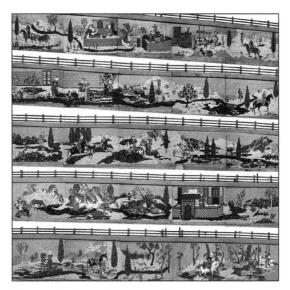

Figure 4 Reza Khodadadi's mural *Naghsh-e Khatere* (lit. 'Memory's Role') extends along the wall of a highway (photo by BT, used with permission)

Former Urban Beautification Organization employee Baran argues that commissioning Tehran's artists to paint brightly coloured murals in diverse locations around the city instils in them a sense of ownership over their city (personal communication, 12 February 2008). She believes that illuminating dreary landscapes with colourful geometric murals that reflect upon both traditional and contemporary Iran (see Figure 4) connects the city's residents with their neighbourhoods rather than alienating them, which is what the austere images of war and martyrdom seem to have done (ibid.). This shift in how official organizations view the important role public places play in strengthening a sense of community parallels a general trend in the broader society towards awareness of physical surroundings and the desire to claim these on a personal and social level.

The last decade in Iran has seen a movement towards greater freedoms by the people. The state works against this, periodically cracking down on social, cultural and political freedoms. Many outsiders perceive Iran to be a grim place where women are absent from the public sphere, but this is not the case. Today, women comprise over half of new university entrants, are proportionately present in the work force and are politically aware and active. Some young men and women push the boundaries of what is legally acceptable, but the authorities are becoming relatively powerless against the small infringements of everyday life in Tehran. In a country where nearly two-thirds of the population is younger than 30, universities are proving to be fertile ground for dissident ideas and such ideas are becoming increasingly difficult for the regime to control.[11]

The Iranian government is comprised of multiple factions contending for control, which DeBano claims is resulting in 'discrepancies between official policy and life' (2005: 442). Vivienne Walt, an independent reporter writing for *Salon*, states that the rules of the regime have forged two spheres in Iran, the 'official' and the 'real' (2000). Official rules and regulations seem to have very little impact on the private lives of many Iranian people. Much of Iran's social and cultural life was forced behind closed doors after the instigation of the Islamic Republic of Iran but it continued evolving and perpetuated to the point where it began overflowing into the streets. A gradual and general nudging of the rules, particularly by Iran's youth, has meant that over the three decades since the instigation of the Islamic Republic of Iran much has changed. In *Lipstick Jihad* (2005: 61–2) Moaveni states:

> When Iranians stopped to scrutinize exactly how and where these transformations had taken place, they concluded it was from below – in people's behaviour and dress, their ideas, spirits, and conversations, attitudes and activities. At some historic moment impossible to pinpoint, around the turn of the millennium, Iranians' threshold for dissimulation and constriction sank, and people simply began acting differently.

Narrative non-fiction writer Christiane Bird (2002: 11), presaging this, remarked, 'The ground in Iran is constantly shifting. What's true today will not be true tomorrow. And what's true in one town, city, or establishment may not be true in another . . . laws are often elastic and subject to interpretation'.

The 'elastic laws' of the Islamic Republic are impossible to predict. At the end of September 2006, while driving down Shariati Street in a Land Rover with two friends after a party in a villa on the outskirts of Tehran, on what just happened to be one of Iran's 27 annual nationwide religious holidays, I drew out my camera to take pictures of the procession and street decorations. My friends implored me to put my camera away as it would draw unnecessary attention to us on a day when the police and *Basij* (a paramilitary volunteer militia) were known to be particularly strict. I had been on Shariati Street many times before, camera in hand, but a young mixed-gender group that included a foreigner was not something to draw attention to on a day of national mourning. One of my companions said, 'The laws are so vague here that they can arrest you for anything, everything and nothing – all at the same time' (Raz, personal communication, 20 September 2006).

The street we were on was named after Ali Shariati, a sociologist, revolutionary and religious scholar, who was instrumental in the lead up to the revolution. Although he died before the revolution, one of his most famous sayings, quipped in the hope of motivating pious Iranians to revolt against the monarchy rather than to wait for the Hidden Imam to return justice to earth, was, 'Every day is Ashura; every place is Karbala' (in Nasr 2006: 129).

Let's party like it's AD 680

Ashura, a term sometimes interchanged synonymously with Muharram, but correctly describing the tenth day of the month of Muharram, is an annual mourning ceremony held for the prophet Mohammad's grandson Imam Hussein. Imam Hussein was killed over 1300 years ago in the Battle of Karbala (AD 680). In the days leading up to Ashura community groups and some families cook food to donate to others. This act of giving is called *nazri*, a type of alms, and Iranian youth share with each other the best places to get free food. They spend the nights during this month driving all over the city to get the best *nazri*, eating from polystyrene boxes in the streets; through this act of defiance they surreptitiously claim back the public sphere for themselves, at least temporarily.

The police and *Basij* are particularly strict during Ramadan and Muharram, the holiest months of the year, but youth adjust their behaviour accordingly. In fact, Iranian youth have appropriated many of Iran's national holidays and transformed them into social occasions. Street processions occur annually on days like Islamic Republic Day (Persian: *Ruz-e Jomhuri-ye Islami*), the Day of the Victory of the Revolution (Persian: *Ruz-e Piroozi-ye Enghelab*) and Student Day (Persian: *Ruz-e Daneshju*). It would be unusual for a mixed-gender group of unrelated youth to be stopped by police during these processions, providing they weren't doing anything out of the ordinary, as they are state-sanctioned gatherings. The best example of the appropriation of state-sanctioned ceremony occurs during the annual mourning month of Muharram. This month plays host to what is, effectively, a string of street parties sanctioned by the state. In terms of importance, from a social calendar point of view, these parties come second only to *Chaharshanbe Soori* (lit. 'red Wednesday'), a night of fireworks and secular ritual that marks the beginning of the Iranian New Year.

Figure 5 An immense crowd huddled together in the bitter cold to watch the re-enactment of the Battle of Karbala outside Khordad 15th metro station, central Tehran, on the day of Ashura, 20 January 2008 (photograph by author)

Street processions mark the pivotal nights during the mourning month of Muharram. The first time I saw one of these processions I was travelling at a snail's pace down Jolfa Street in a shared taxi on my way home. Wondering why the traffic was more congested than usual, I craned my neck out of the window and found myself jostling with the other passengers for the best view. We saw a group of men of all ages, dressed in black, who were striking their bodies rhythmically with chains, beating big drums and marching in an orderly and sombre fashion. The sound of the street marchers as they passed slowly under the concrete overpass was overwhelming, their metallic chains and gargantuan Yamaha bass drums reminiscent of industrial metal music. While the police are more strict during the month of Muharram, on the nights of public mourning middle-class youth pile into cars, go to watch the festivities, buy food from street-vendors and trade phone numbers on pre-printed paper slips in the hope of finding a new boyfriend or girlfriend – one of the many ironies of the Islamic Republic.

Conclusion

One of the biggest ironies of the Islamic Republic is that the authorities engage in exactly the same types of censorship and suppression as the Pahlavi dynasty did before them. A diverse population of Iranians, frustrated by the king's exertion of power in the public sphere, rose up and overthrew the monarchy, ending more than 2500 years of dynastic rule. They saw his attempts at modernization to be detrimental to Iranian culture and revolted against social injustices and the increasing divide between the rich and the poor. Many of these social injustices have since been repeated in the Islamic Republic. Their constitution is full of literary loopholes that allow them to bend or re-interpret the rules according to context and need. My research has shown that the ruling regime's 'fundamental principles of Islam' are fundamentally different from those of pious Iranians. If the constitution would only delineate what these principles are, then people would have an easier time abiding by them.

But this is not the only issue. The authorities, as they jostle for power, are unable to agree on what should be permitted. In the next chapter I analyse responses from senior Iranian clerics to a question I asked them concerning the appropriateness and acceptability of music from an Islamic perspective. Although state forces mediate the public sphere rigorously, this chapter has shown how the Iranian people have gradually fought for more freedoms in public in spite of these restrictions. Far too complex to cover in a brief overview, Iran's political history has very much affected the social and political environment in which unofficial rock musicians currently live. At times it seems like no expression made in Iran can be apolitical, which is why it was so important to give a socio-political overview relevant to the research topic at the beginning of this book. The reader is referred to more comprehensive sources in the endnotes, but should have a good under-standing of how intrusive the rules of the Islamic Republic are on the lives of ordinary citizens.

Notes

1 See Sedghi's text for an overview of 'veiling, unveiling, and reveiling' in Iran (2007).

2 See Kinzer (2003) and Pollack (2004) for texts about American–Iranian relations in the 1950s. Diba (1986) and Gasiorowski and Byrne (2004) discuss Prime Minister Dr Mohammad Mossadegh's brief but popular time in power and his overthrow by the CIA-executed, MI6-sponsored coup called 'Operation Ajax' in 1953. Seliktar (2000) and Bill (1988) also provide pertinent historical accounts of Iranian–American relations.

3 Shahidi (2007: 17) demonstrates how the power of SAVAK decreased over time as it softened its approach to the press while the Shah's regime fell apart. When the Shah's power was strong SAVAK dictated the printed content of Iran's newspapers, but by 1979 SAVAK merely contacted papers requesting them to print corrected reports when they deemed necessary.

4 For more information about the different political parties vying for power in the lead-up to the 1979 revolution see Fazeli (2005), Poulson (2005), Kurzman (2004), Tachau (1994), Chehabi (1990) and Keddie (2003).

5 Playwright and political writer Dilip Hiro provides an excellent account of the months preceding the revolution in *Iran under the Ayatollahs* (1987: 66–94).

6 When the constitution was amended in 1989 the office of Prime Minister was abolished due to the acute tension that had dominated the relationship between the Presidents and Prime Ministers of the Islamic Republic of Iran for ten years.

7 Palizdar, a member of the Iranian parliament's Judicial Inquiry and Review Committee and a fervent Ahmadinejad supporter, was arrested because he accused several high-ranking Islamic clerics of economic corruption.

8 It is likely that these non-uniformed law enforcers were members of the *komiteh*, *Basij* or Revolutionary Guard, whose aim it is to 'safeguard' the morals of the Islamic Republic.

9 See the Urban Beautification Organization's official website, available online in Persian, at http://www.tehran.ir/Default.aspx?tabid=11493&language=en-US

10 In 'Tehran murals embrace new themes', *ABC News* (12 April 2009), available online at http://www.abc.net.au/news/stories/2009/04/12/2541133.htm

11 Iran's total population is 70,495,782. Those aged 0–30 total 42,644,764, which is 60.5 per cent of the population. More than half of those aged 0–30 are older than 15. See the full data from the 2006/2007 census online at the Statistical Centre for Iran's website, http://amar.sci.org.ir/index_e.aspx (new site under construction).

CHAPTER TWO

Music in Iran: from pop to pariah

This chapter begins with an investigation into *tasnif*, a genre of metric vocal music made popular by poets and composers during the latter part of the Qajar Dynasty (1794–1925). *Tasnif*, which was extremely popular in twentieth-century Iran, sometimes incorporated political sentiment into its lyrical texts. The works of Sheida and Qazvini, the most well-known twentieth-century composers of *tasnif*, remain popular today. *Tasnif's* popularity was so pervasive that the word itself is now also used interchangeably with the word 'song' in the context of popular music (Nettl 1992: 54; Ghanoonparvar 1993: 177). Although *tasnif* is a technically a classical genre, its strong rhythmic metre and reliance on poetic text to convey significance make it the logical starting point for an examination of post-revolutionary rock music.[1]

This chapter will conclude with an insight into the musical careers of Googoosh and Vigen, two of Iran's most adored pre-revolutionary pop music stars. These case studies contextualize the situation in which musicians now create. Music was the first art form to be banned in the Islamic Republic, silencing the voices of these idolized pop stars and forcing most into exile. The mass exodus of Iran's pop musicians following the revolution, the estab-lishment of a flourishing popular music industry in diaspora, and the siphoning back of this music through the black market to post-revolutionary Iran laid the initial foundations for the development of the unofficial rock music scene.

Musical monarchies and poetic politics

Through the active promotion and patronage of rulers like Mohammad Shah and Nasser al-Din Shah, music became an integral part of courtly life during the Qajar Dynasty (1794–1925). Although conservative Shi'a rulers had banned music during the Safavid Dynasty (1501–1736), it was revitalized during the Zand Dynasty (1750–1794) and there was an increased demand for musical performances at aristocratic parties during the subsequent Qajar Dynasty. Qajari shahs employed many courtly musicians, particularly those of Turkic origin (Daniel and Mahdi 2006: 198). The shifts in the statuses of music and musicians aligned themselves very clearly with the distinct changes in political authority, and this is still the case. The Qajar Dynasty was the first Iranian dynasty to commission a national anthem, called 'Salamati-ye Shah' (lit. 'wellbeing of the king'), which was composed by the French military musician Lemaire. It was also around this time, although not in the court, that music was first used as a tool for political reform.

The history of pop music in Iran can be traced directly back to the *tasnif* genre. It may be a classical genre, but the popularity of its performers, its strong rhythmic metre and its poetic lyrics distinguish it from others forms of Iranian classical music. Poets and composers like Abolqassem 'Aref' Qazvini (1882–1934) and Ali Akbar Sheida (1843–1906) were the most eminent performers of *tasnif* during the latter part of the Qajar Dynasty. Aref, arguably Iran's first 'singer-songwriter', was a member of the Revolutionist Party, which was fighting for reforms in the Iranian constitution in the hope of stripping away some of the monarchy's power. These reforms were eventually attained after the Constitutional Revolution of 1906. Like any singer-songwriter, Aref composed a large number of songs with romantic themes, but revolutionary and political songs also featured strongly in his corpus. Composers such as Aref and Sheida used poetry effectively to promote their messages to a wide Iranian population (Cronin 2004: 122). Poetry was the most valuable tool for communication at that time, because although a great number of Iranians were illiterate at the beginning of the twentieth century, all of them had grown up in a culture where memorizing and reciting poetry was an integral part of social life.

All of the Iranians I have ever met can recite verses of poetry and most enjoy debating the veiled meanings that have been secreted away in the philosophical metaphors characteristic of Persian poetry. Even the standardized Grade One textbook, used in every first-year classroom across the country, teaches its moral and spiritual lessons through poetry. There is a common Persian saying that translates, 'Even the poorest households have two books, a copy of the Quran and a copy of Hafez', and many homes have multiple editions of both. Hafez (1350–1390) is arguably the most famous of the classical Persian poets. Greenberg argues that Hafez is Iran's equivalent to Shakespeare, and that the *ghazal*, his chosen genre, is structurally similar to the sonnet (2008: 461–2). But Hafez's popularity has endured more strongly across the generations than Shakespeare's, and his poetry appeals to a far broader social spectrum. In addition, the *ghazal*'s structure is far less defined than that of the sonnet.[2]

Iranians treat Hafez as a prophesier, opening his collected works at a random page to allow him to divine a fortune based on a pressing question recited silently. In bazaars and on street corners children hawk embellished paper envelopes containing a verse of Hafez (see Figure 6). The customer recites a question or thinks of a person's name while selecting an envelope, and the verse inside becomes a prophecy relating to whatever was thought about during the selection process. Some hawkers train budgerigars to select the verses for the customer. Poetry is so ingrained in Iranian society that it was bemusing rather than surprising when a *fa'al-e hafez* (lit. 'Hafez's fortune') was delivered to me direct by motorcycle one day, attached to the inside of a pizza box lid.

Informal poetry clubs are held regularly in homes across Tehran and to be invited to one is a privilege. These poetry clubs are just some of the many informal, unofficial gatherings that happen inside Iranian homes, away from the gaze of the state, for the purposes of education or entertainment. The importance of the Quran and Hafez's poetry in Iranian households, the pivotal texts of religion and poetry, says something very particular about Iranian culture. 'Hafez', a name given to someone who has memorized the Quran, was a religious man who practised Sufi mysticism, but he wrote many poems incorporating imagery of both love and wine. This imagery, often in conflict with Islam, is symbolic and ambiguous, lending various meanings to the poems in various contexts, in turn strengthening their power, passion and far-reaching appeal.

Figure 6 A young boy selling Hafez's fortunes in Tehran Bazaar, 2006 (photograph by author)

A full overview of both poetry and folk music is too vast to broach adequately within the remit of this book (see Karimi-Hakkak 1995 and Thackston 1994), but the main argument made here is that the histories of politics and poetry in Iran are intertwined. Poetry can have a strong impact on the shaping of ideals and can also be used as a political tool. Keshavarz argues that poetry was 'viewed as a central tool for social reform' by the mid-twentieth century in Iran (2006: 136). One of the poets that contributed to this poetic awakening was Nima Yushij (1897–1959).[3] Although the works of his successors were more politically overt, Nima is attributed with reinventing the content and form of Persian poetry, both of which had been strictly defined for centuries (see Bashiri 2000). It took a great deal of time for Nima's radical modernist poetry to be accepted by general society, but he was instantly popular with a number of young poets that had aligned themselves with the Tudeh party (Ostle 1991: 149). Through an examination of the Islamic government's staunch opposition to music in the unstable first years of the Islamic Republic in the next chapter, it will become obvious that this stricture was due in part to music's connection to politics throughout history.

Soheil Nafisi, a self-taught and experimental contemporary folk musician, recently reworked one of Nima's most politically provocative poems. I first heard the recording of 'Oh! Humans',[4] Nafisi's interpretation of Nima's 'Ay Adam-ha', in a fashionable Tehran coffee shop and was immediately attracted to its sparse and melancholic style. Nafisi and Hermes had successfully applied for permission to record and release this album, which was permissible because of its slow and sparse rhythms, Persian lyrics and heavily veiled metaphors. Nafisi, born in Tehran in 1967, spent more than 20 years of his early life living near Bandar Abbas, the capital of Iran's Hormozgan Province.

The eclectic Bandar Abbas has been Iran's most important trading port for centuries (Dumper and Stanley 2007: 69–72). The musical styles imported to Iran's southern port by traders and slaves from places as diverse as India and Africa have audibly influenced Nafisi. He composes his songs around the texts of poets such as Nima, but they have a folk quality to them that inspired his record label Hermes to call his music a kind of Iranian Chanson. Nima's poetry, which uses symbolic imagery to speak covertly about the tyranny and injustice of the Pahlavi Dynasty and about the poverty and ignorance of the people, suits Nafisi's sullen vocal delivery. The time chosen by Nafisi to release his resurrection of 'Oh! Humans' seems symbolic: was he intending to speak out against another type of tyrannical rule? The year was 2005 and Ahmadinejad had just taken office.

Excerpt of lyrics from Nafisi's 'Oh! Humans', an abridged version of Nima Yushij's poem of the same name, translated by the author:

Oh! Humans,
Sitting happy and laughing on the shore
Someone in the water is dying
Someone is beating his hands and feet
Against this angry, heavy and dark sea

'Oh! Humans' describes a group of people watching calmly from the shore as somebody struggles to keep their head above a tumultuous body of water. The phrase 'Oh! Humans' (Persian: *Ay Adam-ha*) is threaded through the composition, beginning each verse and ending the song on faded repeat. Nima Yushij, like his contemporaries, relied greatly on symbolic imagery to develop his philosophical and political ideas because the Pahlavi Dynasty was so restrictive.

In the text of 'Oh! Humans' the narrator, perhaps a political instigator, calls upon a disengaged society to act against tyrannical rule. A metaphorical reading sees the ocean as the dictatorial regime and the person drowning as the only one who was brave enough to speak out. The observers feign ignorance, watching in a disaffected state of complacence. Nafisi sings, 'Oh! Humans, enjoying yourselves, sitting on the shore, bread on your tablecloths and clothes on your backs, someone in the water is calling you'. Although Nima Yushij and Soheil Nafisi are from different generations and were raised in different social and political climates, the poem's original message remains resonant in the Islamic Republic. Nima Yushij, a leftist, was deplored by the monarchy, which prevented many of his early poems from being published. It wasn't until after the fall of Reza Shah and the establishment of *Ahang* (lit. 'music'), a magazine with Yushij on the editorial board, that his work became widely known.

The bond between poetry and music is inseparable and the histories of both are fraught with tragedy. Fereidoon Farrokhzad, the brother of Iran's most beloved female poet Forough, was as controversial in life as he was in death. Dr Fereidoon Farrokhzad, political scientist, poet, TV host, actor and singer, and outspoken opponent of the Islamic Republic of Iran, was found in a pool of blood at his home in Germany on 6 August 1992, aged 55. Three days earlier he had been stabbed multiple times and beheaded. His dog was found waiting patiently beside him. Fereidoon was Iran's Jules Holland. In the late 1960s he had hosted a variety show on television called '*Mikhakeh Noghrei*' (Silver Carnation) through which he discovered many of Iran's most famous musicians. In 1979, along with dozens of other singers and actors, Fereidoon was summonsed to appear in the Revolutionary Court. He was imprisoned and fled to Germany upon his release. Amongst the dozens of glamorous superstars performing to aristocrats, the intelligentsia and expatriate workers in pre-revolutionary Iran's hotels, nightclubs and seaside resorts, two of those who shone most brightly were Googoosh and Vigen.

A history of pop music in Iran

Googoosh, one of Vigen's students, was one of the last pre-revolutionary pop stars to flee Iran, hiding silently for more than 20 years after the instigation of the Islamic Republic before making her escape. Prior to the revolution, pop music was a lucrative industry in Tehran and its popularity was founded mainly by Vigen Derderian (1929–2003), an Armenian-Iranian singer. Vigen sang in both Armenian and Persian and, like most of Iran's other pop stars, also featured in several popular movies. His recording career began in the 1950s, after he had gained popularity by performing in live and pre-recorded radio broadcasts. Vigen was one of the first Iranian musicians to bring the guitar into his performances (see Figure 7). After buying a guitar from a Soviet soldier, Vigen moved with his family to Tehran in 1951 and secured his first regular gig playing at Café Shemiran in the northern suburbs of Tehran. Shemiran was, and still is, a playground for the rich. Sadeq Saba, in an obituary for Vigen published in the Guardian, claimed he targeted the new youth market cleverly in the 1950s and 60s and became the country's first pop star after decades of a music industry dominated by traditional singers like Aref and Sheida.

The start of Vigen's career conveniently coincided with the emergence of an archetypal middle class in Iran, much in the same way that the start of Elvis' career coincided with the emancipation of a generation of teenagers in the US. Vigen performed and recorded more than 600 songs and worked with many established Iranian lyricists and musicians over the span of his career. In addition to Café Shemiran, Vigen performed at some of Tehran's other hotspots: Café Astara and Café Jahan in Tajrish, and Moonlight Park, which was owned by the Iranian diva Delkash (Javid 1997). '*Mahtab*' (lit. 'moonlight') was the first song that Vigen performed on the radio in 1951. Radio technology, as discussed below, played a large part in the spread of new music genres in Iran; television was not broadcast in Iran until 1958.

As the media industry developed and the Shah's attempts at modernization and promotion of the foreign took hold in Iran, traditional music began to wane in popularity (Daniel and Mahdi 2006: 200). Iranian television was established in 1958, the University of Tehran's Music Department was opened in 1965, the Iranian Centre for Preservation and

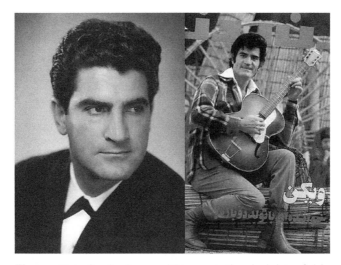

Figure 7 Left: A dapper Vigen at the height of his career. Right: Vigen on the cover of *Zan-e Ruz* (*Women of Today*) magazine in the early 1970s. He is juxtaposed against a background of rural women wearing brightly coloured headscarves and robes.[24]

Dissemination of National Music in 1968, and the Institute of Musicology in 1973. Although the latter two institutions encouraged the preservation of folk, traditional and classical Iranian music, pop music pervaded television broadcasts and the University of Tehran's Music Department focused on training musicians in western art music. One of the Shah's main goals was to promote the arts, which he did mainly for political ends (see below). Perhaps he was encouraged to be a patron of the arts by his wife, Empress Farah Pahlavi, who was a great art enthusiast.

Empress Farah inaugurated numerous organizations that brought traditional and contemporary Iranian art to prominence both inside Iran and in the western art world. She entrusted her cousin Kamran to build Tehran's Contemporary Art Museum, which to this day has paintings by artists such as Picasso, Francis Bacon and Andy Warhol secreted away in its vaulted basement. In 1970 and 1971 the Ministry of Culture and Arts was allocated 543,179,000 IRR to promote the arts. While this was a substantial sum of money in those days, it was only 1 per cent of the GNP. Of the Ministry of Culture and Arts' budget, 23 per cent was spent on administration services, 16.41 per cent on protecting monuments and archaeological sites, 17.93 per cent on art education programmes, and 42.66 per cent on the 'dissemination of culture' (Djamehid 1973: 22). With the money, the Ministry of Culture and Arts established networks of urban and rural cultural centres (32–3) and encouraged the production of new films in order to exert cultural influence by 'presenting new patterns of attitudes and ways of life to a society in transition' (28). In 1971, Tehran's three radio transmitters broadcast 8,755 hours of music, approximately eight hours each per day. Radio Iran played 93.1 per cent Iranian music and Radio Tehran broadcast 11.3 per cent (Djamehid 1973: 35).[6] A 1971 survey estimated that there were two million household radios and that each radio had an average of four regular listeners (42). The population of Iran in 1971 was approximately 30 million, which means that nearly a third of all Iranians listened to the radio at that time. The radio is still a popular broadcast medium in today's Iran.

Many other musicians became popular performing similar songs following Vigen's performances on national radio. These performances transformed him from a relatively unknown musician into an instant superstar among Iran's middle and upper classes. Vigen and his contemporaries performed with small orchestras or backing bands and they seldom wrote their own songs. The solo singer of pre-revolutionary pop music poses a stark contrast to the group ethos that characterizes Iran's unofficial rock music scene, a theme that will be discussed at length in the subsequent chapters of this book. For nearly 30 years following Vigen's first radio appearance the pop music industry grew exponentially. Googoosh, one of Vigen's students and contemporaries, became the quintessential Iranian diva. A description of her career will lead this chapter into the discussion about the controversial status of music within Islam, the banning of music by the Iranian government in 1979, and the mass exodus of pop musicians to California's sunny shores.

Googoosh (b. 1950), born Faegheh Atashin, began performing as a paid professional at the age of three, alongside her father who was an acrobat and itinerant entertainer. She was my first introduction to Iranian music. It was her cassette that I heard in the rusty green BMW that was being driven by my first Iranian friend Manouchehr. Googoosh's song 'Gol bi Goldoon' (lit. 'flower without a vase') was so enchanting that it inspired me to learn the Persian language, if only to understand what she was singing. Googoosh's music has proved timeless and is still popular in Tehran today. Googoosh was creative and adventurous, and many women followed her styles religiously (see Figure 8). Kamran, a 40-year-old multi-instrumentalist who lives in a humble apartment in Tehran with his mother, remembers Googoosh and his introduction to pop music in the following statement:

> At the beginning of the revolution I was 10 years old and Iranian pop music was really just coming into the forefront. We had Googoosh, Dariush, Ebi . . . In my opinion they gave us some really beautiful pop music, because before that we just had traditional music . . . And it was about that same time that pop music was becoming really big throughout the whole world . . . I really liked pop music, because that was all there

Figure 8 The album cover for Googoosh's record Epitaph. Googoosh was a trend-setter; when she cut her hair short, scores of young women rushed to the salons to copy her new style. Her outfits were themed, sometimes sophisticated, sometimes sassy, and they always pushed the boundaries of fashion in Iran. She invented her own style of dancing, and is sometimes referred to as the Madonna of Iran.

was for us at that time. In my opinion they were playing great concerts, but then came the revolution and pretty much everyone left. (Interview with the author, 1 July 2008)

And 'pretty much' all of Iran's pre-revolutionary pop stars did leave before or shortly after the revolution. Googoosh was an exception. She was outside Iran at the time of the revolution and, despite being warned against doing so by friends, she returned to Iran shortly thereafter. Upon arrival at Tehran's Mehrabad Airport, her passport was confiscated and she fled the airport in a taxi. A short while later she was imprisoned for three months for living out of wedlock with her lover Homayoun Mestaghi. When she was released from prison she became a social recluse. Afraid to leave her own home, Googoosh became a virtual prisoner in the newly founded Islamic Republic of Iran. Unable to sing for 20 years due to the new laws set in place by the Islamic government, Googoosh remained a nostalgic idol until her eventual departure in 2000.

When the newly formed government of the Islamic Republic of Iran set about eradicating all traces of the monarchy, pop music bore the brunt of their new policies. Those musicians who either chose to remain in Iran or were unable to leave were summonsed to the new revolutionary court and forced to sign a declaration promising to abandon their careers and never perform again. Musicians like Giti Pashaei and Koroush Yaghmaei may have re-established their careers in the Islamic Republic but they had to make a number of compromises. Yaghmaei, the grandfather of progressive rock and psychedelic music in Iran, began life as a classical musician. He was 10 years old when his father gave him a *santour* (Persian dulcimer) and he dutifully studied traditional Iranian music for five years before getting his hands on his first guitar aged 15. Unlike most of Iran's pre-revolutionary superstars, Yaghmaei elected to stay in Iran after the revolution and suffered under the vow of silence imposed by the Islamic regime. He whiled away the time publishing children's stories. Although he was able to begin recording his music again a tiresome 17 years after the revolution, it was a further seven years before he was permitted to publish a photograph of himself on any of his album covers. Giti Pashaei, a cabaret style singer who oozed sophistication, survived in Iran after the revolution by composing film scores. She was married to film-maker Masoud Kimiai before being diagnosed with cancer. While Giti was undergoing treatment for her cancer in Germany, she was told that Masoud had scandalously deserted her in favour of Googoosh, whom he later married. Giti abandoned her treatment and returned to Iran, where she died alone and depressed.

Conclusion

Beginning at the end of the Qajar Dynasty, this chapter followed the history of popular music in Iran through some dramatic changes in social, cultural and political context through to its controversial ban at the turn of the revolution. The pre-revolutionary music industry was transformed from pop to pariah in less than a year. Vigen and Googoosh, two of Iran's most famous pre-revolutionary pop music stars, influenced a generation of impressionable teenagers, but were silenced by the government of the Islamic Republic after the Shah's downfall.

The policies of various Iranian governments have always been central to music's history. The Shah's policies on music and social reform, which arguably led to his demise, affected the whole nation. His promotion of pop music and his attempt to 'modernize' Iran happened at the expense of some of Iran's national arts. Instead, many Iranians perceived his version of 'modernization' to be 'westernization'.

The next chapter will begin by investigating why music was so abhorred by the Islamic Republic and follow its journey back from the brink. From music as pariah to today's convoluted mix of pre-approved government-sanctioned pop and 'Satan-worshipping' (Persian: *shaytaan parast*) rock bands (to use the rhetoric of the Iranian government), music in Iran, 30 or so years after the revolution, is certainly a complex affair.

Notes

1 The reader is referred to Tsuge 1991, During 1991, Farhat 1990, Zonis 1973 and Nettl 1987 for in depth examinations of Iranian classical music, which is directly interlinked with classical Persian poetry but is beyond the remit of this book.

2 This statement may prove controversial but I have never yet met a young Briton who carries a copy of Shakespeare's sonnets around in their satchel, unless their high school or university reading lists had prescribed it. Young Iranians are as enamoured of Hafez as their parents and grandparents and own multiple copies of his collected works. Concise copies are mass produced by publishers and carted around in purses, satchels and backpacks to be consulted when required.

3 Iranians consider Nima, born near the Caspian Sea in the north of Iran, to be the father of modern Persian poetry. Other revered poets, like Shamloo for example, were particularly impressed by his style (Anushiravani and Hassanli 2007: 152). The dramatic shift in poetic style that Nima instigated occurred after World War II, when poets had become dissatisfied with the rigid structure of traditional poetry. Above all, this new style was free of the centuries-old constraints of rhyme and rhythm (Daniel and Mahdi 2006: 79).

4 Rira, 2005, Hermes Records HER027.

5 According to the Iranian Law for Supporting Authors, Composers and Artists (Persian: *Ghanoon-e hemayat-e hoghoogh-e mowlefan va mosannefan va honarmandan*) the photographs of Vigen and Googoosh are in the public domain because their term has expired. A photograph's copyright lasts only 30 years from the date of publication. See http://www.nlai.ir/Default. aspx?tabid=729 for further details.

6 Radio Tehran was launched in 1940 and Radio Iran was launched 1957. The British Standard Co. was commissioned to make two short wave transmitters and the Ministry of Post and Telegraph ordered the construction of a building in central Tehran that would house the studio and a wireless telecommunications centre. Some radio shows were so popular that the streets were deserted as they went to air. A vast majority of the shows were music oriented. This information was gleaned from 'History of Radio Iran', at http://www.iranradiofestival.ir/en/GeneralInformation/HistoryofRadioinIran/ tabid/212/Default.aspx which is unfortunately no longer available.

CHAPTER THREE

Music and Islam

Whether or not music is acceptable in Islam is a longstanding and ongoing debate that has been covered by many scholars.[1] When Khomeini won out over the other political factions vying for control in the aftermath of the Iranian Revolution and formed the Islamic Republic of Iran, music and film were the first cultural forms to be banned. Khomeini had denounced the Shah's cultural and social policies in his sermons from exile and perhaps his real desire in banning music and other art forms was to eliminate any of the residue remaining from the monarchy, or anything that was a part of what the Islamic revolutionaries called 'westoxification' or 'occidentosis' (Persian: *gharbzadegi*).[2]

Although Islamic scholars have always contested the status of music, Shiloah argues that there is nothing in the Quran that concerns music explicitly (1995: 32). It seems that the main reason for Khomeini's ban on music was because of its pervasiveness and persuasiveness. Khomeini, a populist, encouraged the use of music in the form of 'revolutionary songs' to rally people's support prior to the revolution (Daniel and Mahdi 2006: 192). But in the fragile first years of the Islamic Republic he knew it was going to be difficult to maintain a stronghold over the Iranian people, so anything that detracted from the revolutionary ideals was forbidden. Houshang, a politically embittered young musician, relished recounting the following joke for me during our extended focus group interview on 9 July 2008:

> [After the] revolution they announced a total ban on music. A song had been written for Khomeini's return to Iran that went 'Khomeini oh Imam, oh fighter, oh sign of honour, oh sacrificer of thine life for the purpose'. We all sang it in school. [The Islamic government] came out and said music is a sin and forbade everything to do with music. One of our great and quick-witted composers asked boldly, 'so how are we supposed to perform "Khomeini ey Imam" then? With our farts?' But

of course performing that song was ok, *because the government decided that it wasn't really a song.* (Emphasis mine)

Houshang's last sentence, a sort of throwaway comment, is the most telling of the whole anecdote. Music is permissible in Iran as long as it is not against the ideals of Islam as they are interpreted by the clerical regime. Khomeini's anthem, coupled with his cassette-tape sermons, mobilized an entire nation of people against the monarchist regime. But was this anthem 'music'? According to Otterbeck, Islam decrees that music requires the passion of humans, which should be reserved solely for devotion to Allah (2004: 14). In Afghanistan music was also forced underground by a hardline Islamist regime. The Office for the Propagation of Virtue and the Prevention of Vice (austerely similar in name to Iran's Ministry of Culture and Islamic Guidance, which is discussed in depth below) was established in Herat after the fall of the communists in 1992 and it was from here that censorship, in the name of Islam, emanated (Baily 2004: 25).

New laws required professional Afghani musicians to hold a licence specifying the type of material they could perform; when music was broadcast on television a vase of flowers was shown instead of the performers (2004: 26–7). This also occurred in Iran. On Iranian state television male vocalists are now shown, but images containing instrumentalists are either shot from a distance so as to render the instrument and performer unrecognizable or are blurred out with camera effects or animations. In comparison, Afghanistan is now in the throes of the sixth season of the highly controversial television show Afghan Star, which is modelled on the American Idol franchise and features both male and female solo singers selected by SMS vote.

Baily argues that music remains 'a sensitive indicator of trends in the broader socio-cultural context' (2004: 27) in Afghanistan, and this is also the case in Iran. As Iranian society has pushed towards more social freedoms, television programming has also become less strict. While this is generally the case, there are still occasional crackdowns on the media, all elements of which are strictly controlled by the conservative Iranian government. Following the 2009 presidential elections Iran's media was heavily restricted and television and radio in particular were used to reproach the protesters and reformist politicians. Kahn-Harris argues that when media is censored, the censor (the Ministry of Culture and Islamic Guidance in this case) inadvertently acknowledges the importance and social significance of the medium it is trying to control (2003: 81). This argument is particularly pertinent when considering the outright banning of music after the establishment of the Islamic Republic and the periodic crackdowns on music, art and entertainment ever since. At a time when they had not yet exerted full control over the Iranian people, censoring culture and art made it easier for the new Iranian government to formulate a new propaganda for Iran and unfold their Islamic and revolutionary ideals.[3]

Iran has always proved to be a unique case and to find out more about the status of music in the version of Islam that Iran's clerics subscribe to, I put some of Iran's most well-known religious scholars to the test by asking them a very specific question. The question, written in Persian and submitted via email was:

> I would like to know what your opinion about rock music (for example, music with electric guitar, drums, bass and lyrics) is. What types of music are forbidden and what facets (for example, loud sound, heavy rhythm etc.) make it so? How can I know whether a certain song is permissible or not?

Ayatollahs (Islamic religious scholars) are very important figures in the lives of pious Iranians. They have offices and secretaries and followers. One of their main tasks is to interpret the Quran and to disseminate their interpretations to their followers. Sometimes religious scholars interpret the Quran differently from their contemporaries, and this means, referring back to the earlier discussion about the new constitution, that there are varying, co-existing, and equally valid 'fundamental principles of Islam'.

Selecting the right scholar to follow is a matter of personal choice (conservative, liberal, reformist) and religious scholars are on hand to answer any questions concerning the Quran and Islam that their followers may have. Modern technology has accelerated this process. All of Iran's respected ayatollahs have their own websites and followers are invited to submit their questions via electronic forms. I submitted my question and was somewhat surprised when the replies began appearing in my inbox. Ayatollahs Ardebili, Gorgani, Sistani and Jannaati all gave similar responses and all of these responses were typed and formulaic except for Ardebili's. Ardebili's office scanned a handwritten note and emailed it to me on 25 August 2009.

Ardebili's reply (see Figure 9) reads, 'Listening to any kind of contrived music, that which is suitable for amusing and fun parties for example, is not permitted and you must judge this for yourself based on the rulings made by your trusted religious scholar/expert'. The only response that differed markedly from those mentioned above was Ayatollah Saanei's. Saanei, a favourite cleric among young Iranians, has his own YouTube channel featuring his sermons and is the subject of a documentary by *Newsweek* reporter Maziar Bahari. Saanei replied, 'If the music is not anti-religious or satanic or futile and if it is not for a mixed-gender gathering where there will be dancing then it is not forbidden and there is no problem concerning it' (personal communication, 11 August 2009). While his religious decrees do prove popular with young Iranians, unofficial musicians are wary of

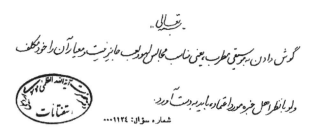

Figure 9 A handwritten response from Ayatollah Ardebili regarding music in the Islamic Republic of Iran

hoping for anything better than their current situation. As singer and guitarist Pouriya noted after reading Saanei's statement, 'It is good in principle but it's just too general. They can still beat the shit out of any musician just according to that statement' (personal communication, 14 August 2009).

Pop music and illegality in the Islamic Republic of Iran

In interviews, unofficial rock musicians depicted early post-revolutionary Iran as a fearful and shadowy place, where much of a musician's or music enthusiast's life was forcibly conducted in private. Being any kind of musician in the 1980s and early 1990s was much harder than it is now. Interviewees spoke of having their instruments confiscated at parties, struggling to acquire good quality illegal cassette tapes, and having their Walkman confiscated at school or in the street. Many of their parents burned whole LP collections out of fear of the new regime, which was also gaining a reputation for its violent imposition of the new rules and regulations. One young man described the tragic fate of a friend who had tried to escape the police during a raid on a party. He was fleeing across the neighbour's roof and crawled across a glass panel that shattered, propelling him to the bottom floor where he died on impact. Despite the ongoing illegality of rock music and the risks involved for those who choose not to abide by the laws of the Islamic Republic, it has never been completely eradicated. It may have retreated behind closed doors, but it fermented quietly in some of the Islamic Republic's private spaces until some more general social reforms, the development of an official pop music industry and the increasing availability of the internet provided an opportunity for 'underground' music to surface, albeit in a limited capacity.

> Rock music was always in Iran. It never got wiped out. Maybe it was in bedrooms for 15, 20 years, but it was always here. (Shahab, interview with the author, 10 July 2008)

The government of the Islamic Republic empowered music by censoring and restricting it. The musicians that I spoke with argued that when it was difficult for them to acquire recordings of music, and even more difficult to practise and perform music, it had a real 'value'. Groups of friends would gather together in secret to listen to a recently acquired recording of Paco de Lucia, Iron Maiden or Pink Floyd and would feel that they were doing something particularly worthwhile, because it was so forbidden. Listening to pre-recorded music was a more social experience during this time, because good recordings were so scarce they had to be shared. Today the young people who walk Tehran's streets do not look so different from their counterparts in the world's other cosmopolitan cities. Many have the latest android phones or personal MP3 players and listen to music as they commute. Iran's closed music industry and relaxed approach to copyright means that even today an original CD recording by a banned artist (some recordings of western jazz, classical music and instrumental versions of pop songs are permitted in Iran) attracts attention at a party; Iranians seldom see a jewel case, album notes, or indeed anything other than a burned CD with a title emblazoned on it with marker pen. When I returned to Iran to visit I took with me a handful of CDs and books for friends. There was never any concern about being stopped with this material, foreigners enjoy certain privileges at Iran's borders, and the look of awe and appreciation as a friend ripped open the cling film surrounding the case and shoved the CD into his or her car stereo was thanks enough.

> Before the MP3 phenomenon took over Iran, there were people older than us who weren't musicians at all but who were collectors of music. They were collecting tapes. And to get a copy of these tapes you pretty much had to kill yourself. I remember that I was out until two in the morning with a friend just to get a copy of *Power and Passion* by Eloy when I was 17 years old . . . Music was really worth something. If you grow up in London and want to listen to Eloy, the reality is that you get the money and go buy it . . . You go into Virgin or EMI or some big place and you find it, but back then we had to earn it. (Pay Mann, 7 July 2008)

Today Iranians download new music and store it on their hard drives. Personal MP3 players are relatively cheap and nearly every car, no matter how decrepit, has an MP3 CD player. Bootlegged CDs of illegal music are sold in queues for the petrol pumps to those who do not have the technology or are not savvy or patient enough to download it for themselves. While it was unheard of for taxi drivers to play illicit music in their vehicles a decade ago, it has become commonplace today. The risk of consuming popular music has been severely minimized because it has become impossible to control. How did music's status change so dramatically over 30 years? Singer and songwriter Houshang, musing on how his musical life has been shaped by his mother's changes in political allegiance over the last few decades, shared the following story:

> Our family was really religious. Music was totally *haroom* [religiously prohibited] . . . my early understanding of music was religious prayers and recitations of the Quran . . . I found a cassette of Fereydoon Foroughi [a popular singer from the 1970s who had written songs in support of the revolutionary movement] in the basement and I brought it into the house secretly. I would play it when dad was out and mum was asleep . . . Then a series of events occurred in Iran that opened up public life and also the mindsets of religious families a little . . . I assembled computers in the bazaar to earn my own money and bought a guitar for myself . . . I left it in the basement and I went down there and to practise it in secret, and I secretly went to lessons . . . Finally one day I summoned the courage to show my mum the guitar. She sat down next to me and cried and confessed that she'd had a guitar before the revolution and that she'd smoked cigarettes! Look, the first time my mum went to see the Imam [the tomb of Imam Reza in Mashhad], she went without a *hejab*, in a blouse and skirt, which totally unheard of, even before the revolution . . . Five or ten years down the line my mum started wearing a chador . . . But now when I play guitar my mum listens. (12 June 2008)

Houshang wanted this personal anecdote to demonstrate how the general social consciousness has experienced many shifts over the last few decades. His mother, a trendy, fashionably dressed teenager who smoked cigarettes and played guitar before the revolution, transformed into a chador-wearing pious woman opposed to music after the founding of the Islamic Republic. As a teenager Houshang was forced to hide his musical aspirations from his mother, unaware that he was mirroring her own youth. Ironically, his mother's shift back to a more secular social consciousness may be due to a generalized disaffection with the Islamic Republic rather than with Islam itself.

Many of the religious Iranians that I spoke with expressed dissatisfaction with the ruling regime and although the rules have changed very little since 1979, Iranians have carved out some semblance of reform for themselves. Today musicians carry their instruments proudly in the streets, not only classical but rock instruments, an act that would have been unthinkable before the late 1990s. Shops along Baharestan Avenue in the centre of the city sell musical instruments and equipment; electric guitars and drum kits sparkle in their window displays, a stark comparison to the gloomy first years of the Islamic Republic.

One of the most dramatic changes to have occurred in Iran was the official sanctioning of certain kinds of pop music at the start of Mohammad Khatami's presidency in 1997. Up until this point Iranians had continued their consumption of popular culture, but were unable to do so in the public domain. While music was certainly played, and the classical music of Iran enjoyed a resurgence of popularity because it was the first form to be permitted again, the government's official ban on popular music ensured that the genre was not present in the public lives of Iranians. The election of former Minister of Culture Hojjatoleslam Mohammad Khatami to the position of Iranian President in 1997 led to a large number of reforms in the cultural sector. For the first time after the revolution certain types of pop music became legalized.

The new Iran-produced and approved pop music blends the futuristic disco beats of House music and the digitized orchestral bank of the Korg keyboard with bland and unprovocative texts. Unofficial rock musicians loathe this pop music even though most of them listen and dance to similarly asinine music produced in the Iranian diaspora when they have had a few shots of *aragh* (a distilled alcohol).[4] While unofficial musicians may not like it, the new official pop music is extremely popular in Iran. Iranians like it because it is sung by singers experiencing their everyday lives, not those who are disconnected from the socio-cultural context of Iran, singing, performing and recording in the US. This new music is also available to everyone, including those without internet connections. Books and CDs are relatively cheap in Iran, as they are subsidized by the government.

In the shadows of an Islamized pop industry

The theocratic regime had effectively empowered pop music for 20 years by banning it. By allowing the production and distribution of this music, the regime was hoping to claim back the potency of pop music for their own benefit. In light of this, the following question posed by Nooshin becomes very pertinent: 'What happens when a form of cultural resistance is appropriated by those against whom the resistance was originally directed?' (2005a: 232). Why did the Iranian government elect to take control of the popular music industry? First, it was a question of economics. The government realized that there was no way to stop Iranians from consuming pop music produced outside Iran, as they were already doing so in droves despite its illegality. The government decided they could reap the economic rewards of a glitzy pop music scene by establishing one of their own. Secondly, Houshang has another theory and in the quote below he highlights the contradictions he believes to be inherent in Iran's government by describing why the government is supportive of a handful of pop musicians, like the mixed-gender pop group Arian.[5] Their existence is controversial because there are many other groups of the same calibre that are denied permission to record and perform. There is no pop music 'scene', it's just a small handful of musicians who are sanctioned and controlled by the Iranian government.

> If we didn't have Arian Band, it would show that we had a dictatorial government, right? However much you say, 'They [the government] are so restrictive, they don't give anyone permission to play music etc.', Arian is their rebuttal. It's like this one band gives them the right to say, 'We've got pop stars so we're not a dictatorship' . . . A government that's so opposed to music! They even paid for Alireza Assar [an official Iranian pop star] to go to Abbey Road and record with the London Symphony Orchestra . . . I don't even know how much money that cost, but I know that if they gave each unofficial rock group one million IRR [approx 57 GBP], they could record one of their works to a very high standard. (Interview, 9 July 2008)

Alireza Assar, an official Islamo-pop artist, performs quite regularly (by Iranian standards) to packed concert halls.[6] In 2005, a series of Assar's concerts was held in the Shahid Avini Hall at Tehran's Bahman Cultural Centre. The large venue had 1400 new seats installed to ready it for the sold-out concert series but the seats were locked together at the armrests, in order to stop them from moving, and the managers of Bahman Cultural Centre deemed the seating arrangements too close for the comfort of a mixed gender audience. The organizers of the concert were forced to separate every single seat before the audience could be let into the hall (Vatanparast 2005).

The Iranian government and its associates are comfortable reaping the economic rewards of a pop music scene, but they are far less comfortable with the accompanying package, the mixed gender audiences, and the fanatic enthusiasm for certain artists. At the annual Red Bull Skate Competition held in Tehran's Enghelab Sporting Complex (see Figure 10), for example, male spectators occupy one side of the outdoor arena, females the other. DJs play instrumental mixes mundane enough to discourage dancing, while the all-male participants skateboard or rollerblade their way to victory or defeat.

Skateboarding is a relatively new phenomenon in Iran and the annual Red Bull skate competition has helped to foster the development of a skate culture in Iran. The music at the annual Red Bull skate

Figure 10 A graffiti artist preparing one of the ramps for Red Bull's annual skate competition in 2008. The graffiti expo occurs the day before the competition starts, to allow for the paint to dry before skateboarders and rollerbladers drop in on the ramps (photograph by author)

competition, courtesy of a DJ, is deafeningly loud but the audience is seated, as are all audiences at state-controlled entertainment events. This is an attempt to further dissuade spectators from dancing. However, as always, the boundaries are blurred; Iran's religious authorities view rollerblading to music very differently from dancing. When visiting a local roller skating rink I was surprised to find mixed-gender skaters boogying on the tarmac to the Iranian pop music being blasted through the arena's small speakers, which were heaving with the thumping bass. This was considered sport, not dancing, just as Khomeini's revolutionary anthem was not deemed to be music and was therefore permissible. The authorities are more concerned with controlling the population than restricting them, which is just a means to an end. They allow certain freedoms in order to placate the population. Pouriya, reiterating Houshang's statement said:

What do you think the authorities prefer, Islam or power? I think everybody knows they have chosen the latter by now. And if they can use specific music content to further stupefy the people then they will say that Islam permits that specific music. Otherwise, they won't. End of story. (Personal communication, 14 August 2009)

When the Iranian government began permitting certain kinds of pop music, they did so in the hope of diluting the power of the Iranian pop produced in exile, a music that they considered to be decadent and depraved, a mirror of western culture. The regime could not have predicted what happened next: rock musicians, who had been multiplying in the confines of Iran's basements, slipstreamed in the wake of this new official pop music and squeezed into some of the spaces prised open by official musicians.

The new laws governing music in Iran, set in place and enforced by the Ministry of Culture and Islamic Guidance, were ambiguous and allowed for some creative interpretation by unofficial musicians. Clarifications given by one religious authority in Iran are often overruled or reneged upon by another, which creates what Nooshin calls a 'liminal space', wherein people are unsure of what is allowed at any given time (2005a: 242). This lack of clarity creates opportunities for creative subversion. In addition, most of the laws are unenforceable in the private domain, which is where Iranians, 'very adept at resistance after centuries of one form of oppression or another' (ibid.), have their greatest opportunity for dissension.

One very clear and pervasive rule is that which requires musicians to apply for permission from the Ministry of Culture and Islamic Guidance before they can release or perform their work in the public domain. *Ershad* (lit. 'guidance') is the soubriquet of *Vezarat-e Farhang va Ershad-e Eslami* (The Ministry of Culture and Islamic Guidance).[7] This ministry comprises many different departments and, like all governing bodies in Iran, is overseen by the Supreme Leader and the Council of Guardians (who are chosen by the Supreme Leader). If musicians in Iran wish to produce, distribute, or perform their music in public, they must navigate a lengthy application process overseen by Councils of Music and Poetry, two subgroups of the Ministry of Culture.

There are three sets of forms and 24 sheets in total. The first set of forms is for a lyric's permit, the second set of forms is for a permit to hold a concert and the third set is for a permit to release a recorded work on cassette or CD. The first set of forms must be submitted to the Office of Art's 'Unit for the Investigation of Lyrics'. Applicants must state whether the application is for a concert or sound recording and submit both hard and soft copies of the lyrics. They must catalogue the songs and then sign a declaration stating that they have observed 'all application laws, rules, requirements, regulations and directions' and accept that they 'will be held accountable for any instance where violation and indictment has occurred' (translation by the author).

The application forms for recording and performing permissions are even more comprehensive. As with all official documents in Iran, each form begins with the header 'In the Name of God the Almighty'. Persons wishing to apply for permission to stage a concert must submit three copies of a good quality CD or cassette, a typed copy of the pre-approved lyrics, a photograph of the group with their respective instruments, and the appropriate forms. This bundle of forms includes the 'Form for the Information Bank of the Country's Musicians', which requires applicants to disclose a great deal of personal information. As well as being a time-consuming procedure, it is also a very specific mode of surveillance. Unofficial rock musicians do not want to disclose their personal details to a system that will most probably reject them, especially when they can be held accountable at a later time.

While some of the unofficial musicians who took part in the research for this book could perhaps receive a permit for their work, the application process is something none of them has any time or patience for, especially after seeing their predecessors fail. Some first generation bands tried to get permits to release their work but none of them was successful. Some of those who were denied permission, like O-Hum (described below) and 127 (described later in the book), were subjected to heavy state surveillance after their application. Some of the musicians from these bands began playing jazz and instrumental progressive rock music in order to be sanctioned by the state because instrumental music is easier to get a permit for.

Adhering to the guidelines of the Ministry of Culture and playing by the rules, however transitory and arbitrary those rules may be, is the only way that Iran's musicians can make a living out of their craft. However, modern technologies have enabled unofficial rock musicians to bypass the government's time-consuming and demoralizing system. While it takes a number of hours to fill out these forms, deposit money into the ministry's bank account and post the forms to the appropriate places, followed by months of waiting for a verdict, musicians are technologically equipped to write, record and distribute their music via the internet in the space of a day. In a focus group interview with his band, Hassan described why they would never consider applying to the Ministry of Culture and Islamic Guidance for permission.

> We don't even try to get permission [to perform]. The culture minister said something really interesting recently. He said, 'Our recent successes are reflected by the fact that an author who knows that their book won't get permission to be published is no longer bringing it to us'. And he said this as if it were a good thing . . . Well, in many ways he was right. When, as a musician, I'm certain that my work won't get permission, why even bother trying?

'Illusions' of grandeur and rock's rebirth in the Islamic Republic

O-Hum (lit. 'illusions') was the first unofficial rock band to become widely known after the Iranian Revolution. The band formed in 1999, 20 years after the revolution, and their arrival coincided with the integration of the internet into the everyday lives of young middle-class Iranians. O-Hum blended the mystical poetry of Rumi and Hafez with progressive rock à la Pink Floyd and they used classical Iranian instruments such as the *kamancheh* and *daf* in some of their songs.[8]

O-Hum's first concert was at Tehran's Russian Orthodox Church, a place that, like Tehran's foreign embassies, has autonomy over the events it holds on its premises (see Meyn 2007). O-Hum applied three times for ministry approval to release their debut album but permission was denied on each occasion. The band eventually sought alternate means of distribution for *Nahal-e Heyrat* (lit. 'the sampling of wonder', 1999) and released it for free on their website as a way of subverting the regime. It was also available under the counter in certain music stores. The regime counteracted quickly and filtered O-Hum's website, disabling all access for Iranians within Iran. O-Hum had no choice but to release their third album *Aloodeh* (lit. 'infected') via the iTunes music store and on P2P (peer-to-peer) file sharing websites, encouraging those inside Iran to distribute it further among friends and acquaintances with limited access.

What was it that was so questionable about O-Hum's music? Their lyrics were the poetry of classical Persian poets, which is not banned. They featured classical Iranian instruments, which are also not restricted. However, their quickening popularity, their broad appeal, and the fact that they were the first group to surface from Iran's underground, at a time when young Iranians were hungry for new music, made them particularly objectionable in the eyes of the Islamic Republic. Although the government had started supporting its own pop industry, it wanted to ensure that it retained control and O-Hum became a prime target for repression. The group disbanded in 2003; Babak, the bassist, wanted to pursue his own solo career and Shahrokh moved to Vancouver. Shahram continued O-Hum as a solo project until 2009, when he reunited with Shahrokh and began piecing the history of O-Hum together for another album. Their most recent album *E-Hum* is a remix collection of O-Hum's songs from 1999 to 2008. When they disbanded in 2003 their popularity dwindled somewhat, but it has been rekindled since their reunion and the release of their remix album *E-Hum*. Their popularity on Facebook is steadily growing (they have more than 12,000 fans), and musicians who previously disliked the band seem to have a renewed respect for the influence the band has had on the unofficial rock music scene.[9]

Since O-Hum's battle with the authorities, groups performing similar music have received permits to release CDs and perform concerts. The Iranian government's main problem seems to be with musicians having autonomy over their work. If a band records and distributes its own work the government has no way of controlling it so they accept and promote a few bands, which are usually managed by people connected to the government, in order to promote a façade of eclecticism and acceptance. As Houshang said above, 'Look, if we didn't have Arian band, it would show that we had a dictatorial government, right?'

Under conditions where the state monopolizes the conventional forms of political communication and seeks to regulate all forms of artistic expression, it becomes possible for musicians (in particular) to assume a leadership role. The state, in its regulatory role, politicizes musical expression, and music's aesthetics in turn make possible an alternative form of political expression (Rodnitsky 2006: 56). Jerry Rodnitsky argues that musical expression is politicized when the state regulates political communication and artistic expression. If we follow his lead and consider that the politics of music 'is a product of the politics of its context' (2006: 53), then we can deduce that unofficial rock music in Iran is intrinsically political, whether the musicians see themselves as being so or not. Performing rock music in Iran without a permit is to partake in an activity that is vetoed by the ruling powers, and to partake in such an activity, regardless of the content of the lyrics or the philosophies of the performers, is to be oppositionist. Whether this is intentional or not is a different story, and most of the musicians that I interviewed were quick to disassociate their music from politics.

'King Raam', the lead singer of the band Hypernova, musing about whether this form of rebellion against the establishment is a subconscious or conscious subversion, decides, 'I think that every underground musician is *subconsciously* defying the authorities. Because they are in all reality, breaking a stupid law, and even though it's not enforced at all times, it's still a law' (2007, emphasis mine). Rock music's contested status in the Islamic Republic of Iran has inadvertently forced its politicization. Music, even if lyrically apolitical, when produced unofficially and illegally under conditions of suppression and censorship becomes politicized as it embodies the political tensions of its immediate socio-political surroundings. Performers at a private concert or party in Iran do not look upon the event as a means for rallying support to overthrow the regime; they perform to escape from the rigidity of their outside world and to explore alternate ways of existing in a society of suppression. However, the fact that the endeavour that they embark on is illegal in the eyes of the ruling minority means that, as King Raam's article suggested, they are subconsciously making a very political statement even if it is cloaked in a façade of political apathy.

In the same way that the politicization of their sound has been forced upon them, so has their 'underground' status. King Raam writes that to be 'underground', a band must be difficult to access and found through unorganized networks that are 'less reliant upon commercial success' (ibid.). But it is important to stress that the musicians and bands described in this book are only 'underground' because the current Iranian government does not approve of their music and because they have no opportunity to develop a public profile. As mentioned in the introduction, while many of Iran's unofficial rock musicians do use the term 'underground music' (Persian: *musiqi-ye zir-e zamini*) in candid conversations about their scene, most of them are shying away from the label when talking in an academic or philosophical way. The terms 'unofficial music' (Persian: *musiqi-ye gheir-e rasmi*) and 'illegal music' (Persian: *musiqi-ye gheir-e ghanooni*) are better appellations, because these terms acknowledge and reflect upon the political context in which the music is created. One of the biggest problems with the term 'underground' is its extensive history of use. It means so many things in so many different contexts that using it in a discussion about Iran's unofficial rock music scene does not lend any relevant description. As Houshang so eloquently put it:

> Art moves on itself, because it's in the minds of people. If they restrict it from above, it moves underneath . . . 'Underground' means something very different in Iran than it does in other regions where the same word is used. When you aren't permitted to go on stage and perform, then it's really underground. (Interview with the author, 9 July 2008)

Conclusion

The contested status of music in Islam and pop music's association with the pre-revolutionary regime ultimately led to the expulsion of Iran's pre-revolutionary music industry. Incidentally, it was the new Iranian government's acknowledgement of the power of music rather than the contested status of music in Islam that hastened the enforcement of its prohibition. After a few short years the music industry regrouped in diaspora and continued to evolve, albeit with new influences and new audiences.

Khomeini had been happy to use revolutionary anthems to mobilize the nation against the monarchy and to unify the people after the revolution, but he did not consider these anthems to be music. His ban on music has had an immense effect on the shaping of pop music in contemporary Iranian society today.

Realizing after 20 years that pop music could no longer be suppressed, the Iranian government attempted to harness the ideological and financial power of the pop music industry for itself. President Khatami transformed public culture in Iran with his reformist values and this enabled the first generation of unofficial rock musicians to peek out from the 'underground', albeit in clandestine form. Iran's unofficial rock music is intrinsically political, despite the desire of its practitioners for it not to be; its politicization is enforced through the context in which it is produced and consumed.

Although it is possible to approach the Ministry of Culture and Islamic Guidance for permission to record, perform or distribute music in the Islamic Republic of Iran, most of the musicians I spoke with are wary of taking part in a process they are certain will end in rejection. While it is possible to purchase a CD produced by an unofficial Iranian rock band under the counter in certain music stores in Tehran, acquisition of unofficial music has become much simpler than that. Word of mouth and the internet provide the most opportunities for the production, promotion and consumption of unofficial rock music in Iran. The possibilities offered by the internet are explored in the next chapter through a description of TehranAvenue Music Festival 1386, a biennial online music festival for unofficial bands and musicians.

Notes

1 An introduction to the debate about music's status in Islam can be sourced in Otterbeck 2004, Shiloah 1995, Sublette 2004: 10–19, and Leaman 2004: 118–20.

2 Jalal Al-e Ahmad (1923–1969) coined the term *gharbzadegi*, variously translated as 'weststruck', 'westoxification' and 'occidentosis' in his 1962 critique of western influence on Iranian culture (translation printed 1984). The book of the same name was published and distributed clandestinely in Iran, because it criticized the Shah's policies. Al-e Ahmad came from a clerical family and Khomeini embraced his message strongly.

3 Although pop music remained largely absent from the public domain for the first 20 years after the Islamic Revolution, film, classical music and visual arts resurged in popularity and patronage. Film was as contested at the time of the revolution but the new government quickly realized its importance as a propaganda tool and it was appropriated as such.

4 *Aragh*, similar to 'rocketfuel', is a type of homebrewed liquor distilled from raisins. Iran's Armenian Christians, exempt from the Islamic law prohibiting alcohol consumption, are permitted to produce and distribute alcohol amongst themselves and many run lucrative and highly illegal businesses supplying this alcohol to willing Muslim compatriots.

5 Arian Band is the Islamic Republic's first and most famous official pop music group. Arian's videos are played on national television and they have been on international tours. The female vocalists, abiding by the rules, sing harmony

vocals not solo parts, which is prohibited in front of a mixed-gender audience. One of the female musicians also plays guitar and composes for the band. They play only a few concerts a year in Iran and their tickets sell out within minutes.

6 No official concerts are held at all on national religious holidays and during the Iranian New Year and the holy months of Ramadan, Muharram and Safar. Ramin Sadighi, director of Hermes Records, points out that this leaves only seven months for official concerts to be held (see http://www.tehranavenue. com/article.php?id=849)

7 The Ministry of Culture and Islamic Guidance's official website can be found at http://www.iranculture.org/. The site's introductory video features still shots of prominent clerics and politicians. Sound recordings of Khamenei saying 'cultural reform is one of the most important subjects of this country' and 'this organization is the one in charge of this important subject' are played over the slide show. The accompanying music is that song that is not a song—an instrumental version of *Khomeini Ey Imam*.

8 The *kamancheh* is a spiked fiddle instrument, with a similar pitch range to the violin, which is played vertically and held upright in front of the player's seated body. The *daf* is a large frame drum with a single skin. Rings are interwoven around the frame, making the instrument sound a little like timpani embedded in a tambourine.

9 O-Hum's official Facebook page is available online at http://www.facebook. com/pages/O-HUM/18730147300

CHAPTER FOUR

Boulevard of virtual dreams: TehranAvenue's online music festival

TehranAvenue.com hosted an online music festival biennially from 2002–2008. It metamorphosed along the way, evolving from a competition into a showcase. The first competition in 2002 was immensely popular and it attracted a large audience, particularly from outside Iran. By 2008, Iran's unofficial musicians had found other ways of promoting their music, the novelty factor had worn off and other online music websites were vying for audience intrigue. Jaded audiences outside Iran, now privy to music from other, far more exotic and war-torn places, were no longer excited by the prospect of such a festival and the number of website viewers sharply decreased. The festival analysed in this chapter was the fourth and final music event organized by TehranAvenue.

Although the biennial event attracted submissions from Iranian bands and musicians and bands with Iranian members outside Iran, a majority of submissions were made from within the country's borders. This chapter describes the history of the festival before taking a closer look at the 1386 (2007/2008) festival, which went online during the year I lived in Tehran. I entered the festival with my friend Pouriya and describe this process below. In the following chapter case studies of the five most outstanding entrants in the rock category, Gatchpazh, Bijan Moosavi, the Free Keys, the Yellow

Dogs, and Kian, will provide an opportunity to discuss the significance that the festival held for its participants.

TAMF: history and goals of the festival

Sohrab Mahdavi established TehranAvenue (http://www.tehranavenue.com) with the help of a group of young writers in 2001. They wanted to create a virtual space for open discourse and free debate for Iranians based in Iran. TehranAvenue's writers reflect upon subjects as diverse as the completion of Imam Khomeini International Airport to their favourite ice cream spots in Tehran and the website also publishes an entertainment guide, which reviews current exhibitions, films, concerts and books. The online festival's first incarnation, 'Underground Music Competition' (UMC), was an experimental project that elicited a great deal more response than Sohrab Mahdavi, Hesam Garshasbi (the sales director of Hermes Records) and the competition's other organizers had anticipated.

The organizers of this inaugural competition gathered together a panel of ten experts. This panel comprised of five TehranAvenue website contributors, four composers and one music producer. Three of the ten panellists owned or managed small recording studios. The panel came up with a list of 30 bands that they thought would be suitable for the competition and TehranAvenue invited them to submit a demo song for consideration. Of the 30 groups that submitted a demo sample of their work to the panel, 21 were accepted to record their tracks at the studios affiliated with the competition, and these works were then posted online. Audience members were encouraged to download the songs and to vote for their three favourite tracks while the competition was open. Audience votes were amalgamated with the rankings given by the panel of experts and the winners were announced.

Initially, the competition organizers had planned to give studio time to the winners to record an EP. However, the winning band would then have had to apply to the Council of Music and the Council of Poetry for permission to record their songs before going into the studio.[1] The organizers ultimately decided that it would be simpler and benefit more of the artists involved to hold a mini rock festival to showcase the finalists at Tehran's Art University. The Art University was selected as the concert venue because it is not required to apply to the Ministry of Culture and Islamic Guidance for individual permissions for events held on campus. These events must be non-controversial however, as the goings-on of the university are still scrutinized by the authorities and the onsite *Basij* (a volunteer militia, patently loyal to the Supreme Leader of Iran).

Ticket agents sold out well before the date of the show, but it was cancelled at the last minute. The bands were gathered together and a representative from Tehran's Art University informed them that the concert had been cancelled; the words 'Rock Fest' that had been printed on the poster had attracted unwanted attention from the authorities. In an interview with the Iranian alternative music magazine *ZirZamin*, one of TehranAvenue's spokespeople said:

> It is true that the Art University didn't let us pull off the Tehran Rock Fest, but we organized the whole affair all the way to the end, and everything was ready (all four nights were sold out, posters had been distributed, four well-known musicians and music organizers had been invited to speak, etc.). It was a great loss to all of us, both in terms of effort and expenses.

Although universities have the freedom to experiment with different art forms on their campuses for educational purposes, and Tehran's Art University is accustomed to experimentation within its perimeter, the term 'rock' had proved to be too controversial. The organizers had tried to cancel the run of posters and re-brand the concert as an 'Experimental Music Festival', but it was too late. Many of the bands from the inaugural UMC, including the band Fara, who won the competition with their kitschy song '*Pashe*' (lit. 'mosquito'), dissolved afterwards. The only one of the inaugural competition's placed bands to have continued recording and performing music together is 127 (third place).[2]

The first competition was held at a time when the internet first began suffusing the lives of young Iranians. At this time, public internet cafés were still the most popular and cost-effective places to access the internet.[3] Before the UMC, 'underground' bands were so underground that nobody except a small clique of trusted friends and acquaintances knew about them. The internet offered relative anonymity and safety to the participants while enabling the promotion of their work to a vast audience on a technological platform not constrained by geographical or political borders. 127's drummer Yahya expressed the following:

> [Before the internet] there was no way of getting your band known. Not for us, not for any group. The year that the first underground music competition was held in Iran, it was the internet that made it possible. There weren't any real live shows. They put a bunch of songs on the website and people went to it and voted. The internet started this scene. And that's with the internet speed of that time! At 2 kbps it took two days to download one song! (Personal communication, 11 July 2008)

Yahya's statement illustrates two main points. First, Tehran's unofficial rock music scene relies solely on the internet to facilitate the distribution and promotion of their work – there would be no 'scene' without the internet. Secondly, the internet has become an understudy for a live stage in the absence of officially sanctioned settings for performance. The internet mobilizes unofficial rock musicians, enabling them to present new works and interact with their audiences, whether through TehranAvenue's music festivals or through their own websites and Myspace pages. The internet is a mediator, a platform between the musicians and their audience, just like a stage in a live performance. 127's singer Sohrab Mohebbi commented in the documentary *Saz-e Mokhalef* (lit. 'offbeat', dir. Mojtaba Mirtahmasb, 2004), 'Our only nightclub for performing in is our website' (28m15s).

The inaugural competition was more popular than the subsequent festivals, even though the competition was held at a time when internet speeds and limited access to communications technologies in Iran made it far more complicated and time-consuming for audiences to access the works. The competition captivated the attention of such a large audience because it was the first time anything of its kind and calibre had been attempted in Iran. It was novel and it was exciting. The 21 songs of the inaugural festival achieved an accumulative download total of 126,000.

Fast-forward to 2008 and while Visprad's progressive metal song '7 Seconds' was downloaded the most out of all of the TAMF86 entries, it only achieved a total of 445 downloads.[4] Why was there so much interest in the inaugural competition? In 2002, the competition was the only way that unofficial Iranian bands could promote their songs and the TehranAvenue team and the bands themselves had advertised the competition widely through Iranian weblogs, which were also growing exponentially in number at that time. Recently, with bands using online social networking communities like Myspace, Facebook, SoundCloud and even their own websites to promote their music, the need for TehranAvenue's biennial music festival has diminished. 127's Myspace profile, for example, has been viewed more than 80,000 times and their songs have accumulated more than 45,000 'plays' on the built-in music player.[5] Through their relentless promotion of unofficial Iranian rock music, TehranAvenue have made themselves redundant. In a time of musical saturation, a festival like this is just one of the many means of distribution.

TAMF86, a free radical?

TAMF is a field. That which appears in it is neither independent nor bonded. It is a free radical. It is both reactive and proactive. It will only *become* when listened to. (Sidewalk 2005,[6] emphasis mine)

Sidewalk's statement positions the TehranAvenue Music Festival as a prime example of a 'Temporary Autonomous Zone' (TAZ) in practice (Bey 1990). Hakim Bey conceives of the TAZ as an uprising and not a revolution:[7]

> The TAZ is like an uprising which does not engage directly with the State, a guerrilla operation which liberates an area (of land, of time, of imagination) and then dissolves itself to re-form elsewhere/elsewhen, before the State can crush it. Because the State is concerned primarily with simulation rather than substance, the TAZ can 'occupy' these areas clandestinely and carry on its festal purposes for quite a while in relative peace . . . The TAZ is thus a perfect tactic for an era in which the State is omnipresent and all-powerful and yet simultaneously riddled with cracks and vacancies. And because the TAZ is a microcosm of that 'anarchist dream' of a free culture, I can think of no better tactic by which to work toward that goal while at the same time experiencing some of its benefits here and now (ibid.).

The festival is a site of creation that belongs to the members of the scene. This zone of temporary autonomy includes the musicians, the organizers, and an audience made up of the conglomeration of internet users who visit the website and participate in critical reception of the submitted works. Sidewalk suggests that the festival itself, the technology medium or vehicle for the transportation of the music, is meaningless and acquires its significance only when the music is actively listened to. As ethnomusicologists Lysloff and Gay argue, significance is to be found not in technologies themselves but how they are used (2003: 18).

Over time TehranAvenue's biennial event has evolved from a music competition into an online festival, revealing how the technology has been adapted in order to cater to the demands of participants and audience members. Sima Momtahan and Naeem Jebelli both wrote and submitted critical guest reviews about the TehranAvenue Music Open (2005 and 2006 respectively) to TehranAvenue's main website. Naeem had participated in the event and Sima was writing her critique from the point of view of an audience member. Naeem's argument was that the voting system, an arbitrary and unbalanced average combining the votes of a panel of ten experts and an audience vote, with no obvious correlation between the two, was flawed (Jebelli 2006). Naeem contended that those who had a larger pre-existing fan-base and were technologically better equipped had an unfair advantage. Naeem also found the festival to be more like a political campaign than a music showcase (ibid.). Sima was concerned with the fact that the music festival seemed more like a commercial competition and that the professional musicians who were recruited to form the panel of experts were biased towards their own performance genres, favouring those artists whose chance of commercial success was higher.

Sima suggested that a better format would be to divide the competition into genres (Momtahan 2005).

As will be revealed below, the fourth and final biennial music event hosted by TehranAvenue heeded the criticisms cited above and created a non-competitive online music festival for Iran's unofficial musicians. Lysloff and Gay contend that technologies become imbued with social meaning as they attain a history of use (2003: 10). TehranAvenue's event is a perfect example of how a technology can be infused with social meaning over time. Global communications technologies like the internet mean nothing in themselves, yet multifaceted layers of meaning come into play when they are appropriated by users in order to circumvent state control, or indeed restricted by that very state. A simple home computer that has been updated with a new sound card and recording software not only provides an alternative to mainstream music industry practices but transfers the control of the music back to the person or persons creating it. This festival, which takes place through a website designed to circumvent the entire censorship and permit-seeking process set in place for music by the state, is a remarkable example of the significance of a temporary autonomous zone. Technologies are not necessarily extraordinary in and of themselves, but the way they are used in local contexts can uncover complex relationships between state, technology, people and place.

The works submitted to TAMF held significance for their composers and producers prior to submission and acquired new significances as audiences interpreted them in various ways. As discussed in the previous chapters, the significance of poetic texts can completely invert when the context of interpretation is changed. Unofficial musicians, starved of official contexts in which to play their music, treat this music festival and any online file sharing opportunities, as their stage. Nooshin, writing about unofficial rock musicians and their creative subversion of the power structures of the Islamic Republic, notes that the deployment of the internet as a medium for distribution 'clearly demonstrates the opportunities that global technologies offer musicians to enable them to circumvent government censorship and control' (2005a: 260).

In September 2007 a call for submissions was posted on the TehranAvenue website and Iranian musicians (or bands comprising at least one Iranian member) both inside and outside Iran were invited to submit one musical work for consideration. The application form stated that the work should be no shorter than two minutes and no longer than five, and that the song should not address any socio-political issues. The festival was divided into four categories and participants were asked to select the most fitting category for their music: rock, hip-hop, fusion or classical. The rock category, with 26 applicants, was the genre with the most entries; classical, with just four, had the least. Unlike the TehranAvenue Music Open or UMC of previous years, TAMF86 was not a competition; there was to be no panel of experts, no voting, and no prize. Each accepted submission was designated a sub-page of the main website where a picture of the entrant(s) or an image that they had selected, a biography, a 30-second 'snippet file' and a full MP3 of their track was available for the public to download. Audience members were able to use the comments form at the bottom of each page to post their opinions about each song, and the artist could then respond to any questions posed.

This non-competitive system was designed to instigate a forum for discussion, which is severely lacking in the unofficial music scene. The lack of communication and collaboration within the scene leads to distrust and paranoia and a vast amount of criticism of the works of others. The musical works submitted to TAMF86 received their fair share of criticism, particularly from other Iranian musicians. The lack of support within the unofficial rock music scene will be discussed in depth towards the end of this book, as it appears to be hindering its evolution. Ped, a singer and the author of a blog called 'This Winki's' (no longer available online) commented at length on TAMF86 in his piece published on 4 April 2008. An aspiring music critic, Ped listened to all 26 of the songs in the rock category and gave them a rating out of ten. In his overview he wrote:

> I was so embarrassed to hear the bands here and I totally lost my hope. I can only 'wish' for a better future in the next century perhaps. Looks like my fellow Persian musicians have a long road to walk just to reach the starting gate.

What interests me about this statement is that Ped, a 'fellow musician', did not enter one of his own works to TAMF86, yet censures most of those who had the courage to do so. Another musician who had expressed a strong desire to enter the competition in our early conversations argued in retrospect that he had not submitted a work because TAMF86 had nothing to offer him. His negativistic response when I asked why he had not submitted a work to the festival was, 'So, I submit a song, so what? There's no prize, there's no concert and no benefits' (personal communication, 1 June 2008).

Although the festival was not designed to be a competition, the organizers could not resist the temptation to provide some sort of analytical overview of the proceedings. In the absence of a panel of experts and an audience vote, a table of statistics showing the number of full song downloads, page views and snippet downloads for each group was published on the website three months after the festival went online.[8] The high number of full song downloads compared with snippet downloads indicates that Iran's internet technology has advanced to a point where most users were able to download the full song, rather than testing whether or not they liked it first by downloading the snippet file. For the UMC in 2002, the total number of snippet files downloaded by visitors to the site from inside Iran was much higher than full song downloads, whereas full song downloads from outside Iran were higher than snippet downloads.

Even the statistics published by TehranAvenue regarding the number of downloads provide convoluted data for analysis. It is impossible to know how widespread the songs' audience-bases became or even if the songs were enjoyed, as listeners may have downloaded the full tracks and not actually liked them. Those who did like the songs may have distributed them to their friends, bypassing the download process and resulting in an unquantifiable total audience. Both Pouriya and I provided copies of the tracks to those with slower internet connections and it could be reasonably expected that others did the same. The number of downloads does not necessarily correlate with the song's popularity because users must first listen to the song before deciding if they like it or not. Thus, the relationship between 'snippet downloads' and 'song downloads' should be the most interesting figure, as it has the potential to prove how many tested the song and liked it enough to download it. In this case though, there were far fewer snippet downloads than full song downloads, suggesting that most people downloaded the full song without hearing the material beforehand.

Participating and observing

In late December 2007, Pouriya and I received a few excited phone calls from other musicians; word was spreading that the TehranAvenue was about to publish a call for music submissions on their website, and everyone was calling and SMS-ing each other to find out if anyone had any news about the conditions of entry or who would be entering. Mobile phones mediate and facilitate everyday life in Tehran.[9] Pouriya and I had been discussing entering the competition since my first research trip to Iran and during that first fleeting month in 2006 we worked on writing songs in his bedroom studio. When I returned in 2007 our musical friendship evolved rapidly and we met at his house most afternoons after my Persian class to write and record. We were still struggling to find a name for our project, four months into my research trip, when the call for submissions to TAMF86 was posted online.

Using Pouriya's bedroom studio, a PC equipped with a cracked version of Cubase, an arsenal of pirated plug-ins, a two-octave MIDI synthesizer, a guitar, a violin and a pair of stereo-matched Neumann microphones, we recorded a track called 'What Do You Think of Red Pens?' It was a hurried affair that had nothing to do with red pens, except for the fact that the lyrics were written on a relatively clean serviette with one. Pouriya wrote the guitar riff and we worked together on programming the beats. We produced the song with the help of Pouriya's brother Pay Mann, the lead-singer and producer of industrial rock metal band Parazitt, now defunct. As the application deadline loomed we still did not have a name. Pouriya had a flash of inspiration while we were filling in the application form. He told me that there were only two Ginkgo trees in Tehran and he liked the way the word looked spelled out on paper. Although there was no way of verifying exactly how many Ginkgo trees there were in Tehran, I was attracted to Pouriya's sentiment. When we were recording music in his room it felt to me as if we were the only two people in Tehran; his bedroom studio was our temporary autonomous zone. After scrawling a biography onto a piece of paper, we selected a photograph from the series of shots Pouriya's girlfriend Simin, a photography enthusiast and Sooreh University theatre student, had taken of us and put these in a sealed envelope along with the CD and filled-out entry form. We then called a *peyk* (a motorcycle courier) and directed them to deliver our song to TehranAvenue's headquarters. Then we waited, and waited and waited.

We had been told during the application process that TehranAvenue would contact the bands to let them know when they received the submissions, but even after chasing up the submission with a few emails we received no news. Finally, and in true Iranian fashion (things never happen quickly or systematically in Iran), the website went online. The festival was uploaded in March 2008 with holiday wishes for the Iranian New Year. The production quality of the submissions (including our own) was low, but this is because of the substandard conditions in which musicians are recording. In contrast with the entrants to UMC in 2002, who had recorded their songs in studios affiliated with the competition, most of TAMF86's songs had been self-produced. Iran's unofficial musicians record mostly in bedroom studios like Pouriya's. Their computers host gigabytes of volatile pirated software and the ever-present ambience of Tehran's traffic hum poses major issues to the sound recordist. Most albums are self-produced and there is seldom a professional producer or a sound engineer onboard. Musicians have learnt how to record and engineer their own music by default. TehranAvenue's music festival shows the dedication of these musicians and this is far more important than debates about recording or production quality.

Examining the festival's impact means discovering what significance the music holds for those who produce it and how those who consume the music interpret it. Therefore, in the following chapter, where I present case studies of some of the bands that submitted works to the festival, I pay particular attention to the comments left on their TAMF86 pages by visitors to the site, their audience members. Although musicians were asked to refrain from underpinning their tracks with politics, many of the works comment, albeit subtly, on contemporary Iranian issues and life in Tehran. The website's activity was not phenomenal; it did not receive millions of hits. Friends or foes of the groups posted a majority of the comments, but there are some significant observations to be drawn from them. Many of the artists commented constructively and openly on each other's pages and the inclusion of this facility provided something that has been absent in the unofficial music scene since its inception – a public and open forum for debate. It is difficult for scene members to congregate in the same physical location and musicians have very few opportunities to discuss each other's music face-to-face.

Music enthusiast and self-styled music critic Behrooz Moosavi, Bijan Moosavi's younger brother, posted a comment on Ginkgo's page musing disparagingly about the use of English lyrics in Iranian unofficial rock music by way of the following eloquent observation (translation by the author):

> Your music was great . . . But one thing that has come to mind that I have to discuss is the great cultural divide between us [Iran] and Western countries . . . [which] has afflicted us with cultural poverty and sucked us into a huge cultural and social vacuum . . . I think it's the duty of all active artists to carry the weight of reducing this difference and fill the vacuum by dedicating their identity to Iranian culture. And by culture I don't mean traditional culture . . . Iranian music, of any style or genre, when it's created under the rubric of 'Iranian music', should have the colour and smells of Iran, or at least allude to Iran in a way that makes it obvious to a foreign listener that they're listening to a work by an Iranian

Behrooz's comment is a prescriptive moral judgement, and he takes up an argument that was also highlighted by Nooshin in a paper given at the International Society for Iranian Studies conference in 2006. She argued that 127, one of the most well-known Iranian groups, would be more appealing to non-Iranian listeners and have more chance at commercial success outside Iran if they sang in Persian instead of English. As will be discussed in the concluding chapters of this book, Nooshin's assumption was right; there is an increasing trend nowadays for bands to sing in Persian and/or use Iranian imagery in certain aspects of their aesthetic production. Behrooz believes that if unofficial rock musicians inject Iran into their songs they can reverse the negative effects of social and geographic isolation. But what exactly is 'Iran' for young Iranians and what does being 'Iranian' mean to them? What makes a song recognizably Iranian? Can the use of Persian language lyrics make something Iranian? How crucial are the lyrics in conveying identity and intention? The themes developed in the previous chapters showed lyrics to be of utmost importance not only to audiences, but also to the Iranian authorities. In the case studies that form the next chapter I begin to examine what might make something 'Iranian', querying whether or not derivative music with Persian lyrics is perceived to be more 'Iranian' than English language songs with contemporary references to Iranian politics and culture.

Notes

1 Official recording studios could previously only record bands and musicians that had already applied for, and been granted, a permit from the Ministry of Culture and Islamic Guidance to release their music. Following a change in the Ministry of Culture and Islamic Guidance's procedures, musicians are now able to record their works in any studio, before approaching the Ministry of Culture for an official permit.

2 127 also submitted an entry to TAMF86, but it is not analysed here, as their work is examined later in the book.

3 In the early 2000s internet cafés were prevalent and frequently patronized by young Iranians. There were thousands of cafés dotted throughout Iran, in cities and some villages, comprising usually only a few computers. It cost about 50 cents an hour to get online, affordable for a majority of Iranians. When pre-paid internet cards became available to the public, and then from 2006 when restricted-speed broadband became widely available for private consumer use, many of the Internet cafés that had not been forcibly closed in cultural crackdowns by the Iranian government simply went out of business, or became shops that sold pirated software (copyright laws are rather flimsy in Iran), video games and printing services (see 'Iran shuts down 24 cafés in Internet crackdown', available at http://in.reuters.com/article/technologyNews/idINIndia-31010620071216

4 See Visprad's Last.fm page at http://www.last.fm/music/Visprad

5 See 127's Myspace page at http://www.myspace.com/127band

6 'Sidewalk' is Sohrab Mahdavi's pen-name.

7 Hakim Bey is the pseudonym of Peter Lamborn Wilson (b. 1954), an American anti-copyright author and political essayist and poet who has uploaded much of his writing to the Hermetic Library at http://www.hermetic.com/bey/. His pseudonym comes from the Arabic words for 'decision maker' and 'gentleman'. Bey travelled substantially throughout the Middle East in the 1970s and 1980s and spent five years working for the World of Islam Festival in Iran from 1974–1980. Bey left shortly after the Islamic Revolution.

8 The statistical overview of TAMF86 is available at http://www.tehranavenue. com/article.php?id=821

9 Mobile phones used to be expensive in Iran because only one company provided SIM cards. Now competing companies like Irancell and Hamrah-e Aval offer cheap prepaid SIM cards with wide network coverage and many young people are using these instead of the more expensive contract phones. It costs approximately 2 cents per SMS, 8 cents per minute of calling and 10 cents per 800 KB of GPRS data.

CHAPTER FIVE

Inventing identity through significant songs: case studies of selected participants from TAMF86 online music festival

Gatchpazh

There are four letters that are unique to the Persian alphabet and do not appear in the Arabic script. Primary school children are taught an acronym to help them remember which letters of the alphabet are exclusively Persian. The letters, in alphabetical order, are G گ, Ch چ, P پ, and Zh ژ. The word formed when the acronym is sounded is 'Gatchpazh'. This is significant because the band's name, an identity signifier, constructs the band as something that is as idiosyncratically Persian as the four aforementioned letters.

Gatchpazh is an Iranian Indie Rock, Funk and Lo-Fi band.[1] The band's members are Hooman Hamedani (vocals), Hadi Sabet (tenor saxophone), Masood Ahmadzadeh (alto saxophone), Sohrab Hosseini (acoustic guitar), Arash Fattahi (bass guitar and band supervisor), and Pedram Hajibashi (drums). '*Benzin*' (lit. 'petrol'), the song the band submitted to TAMF86, pummels the listener with an energetic and chaotic mix of drones and sirens. Alto saxophonist Ahmadzadeh plays the opening passage's 'siren' on the detached mouthpiece of his saxophone. Droning with rhythmic variety on the note E, the band's electric bass and acoustic guitar provide the harmonic fundament for '*Benzin*'. Vahid Safavi, a friend and fan of the band who wrote their biography for TAMF86, claims:

> [Gatchpazh shows] a high talent for being globally famous with suffi-
> cient audiences worldwide . . . While the task of tailoring Persian
> language for new styles of music became a barrier against the young
> musicians, Hooman [the band's singer] proved that understanding of
> music's spirit is something different than the language problems so he
> used his voice as an instrument . . . Gatchpazh is one of the few bands
> in the country who deserves to be known in the world scale if the source
> of creativity still supplies them with such astonishing materials for
> releasing a complete album with decent record quality. [*sic*] (Original
> in English)

Vahid's biography of Gatchpazh presents a theme common to most unofficial rock musicians, which is their desire to be 'globally famous'. All of the musicians that I interviewed said that it was important for them to be 'global' (Persian: *jahani*). Because there is no music industry to support these bands within Iran, appealing to outside audiences in the hope of commercial success is a more viable option. Vahid's biography also speaks of another difficulty that other musicians expressed in focus group interviews, which is the task of setting Persian lyrics to non-traditional genres. Musicians complain that Persian, which is mainly spoken in iambic or trochaic metre, is difficult to set to rock music in a standardized 4/4. Pavlenko argues that Persian, a syllable-timed language, is much less malleable than English, which is a stress-timed language (2005: 55). Most Persian music is composed in triple meter, or in duple meter with a cross-rhythmic and syncopated feel, which fits the syllabic stresses of the language.[2] In addition, the musicians have had few Persian-language musical influences. They have grown up listening to rock music produced with English-language lyrics and are accustomed to the way that it sounds. They have had to invent their own way of coping with the rhythmic intricacies of the language when writing in Persian.

All of the comments posted on Gatchpazh's page were positive and most recognized and commented on the spontaneity and creativity of the band's work. 'Sara' disagreed with Behrooz Moosavi's observation that Hamedani's voice was tinged with the grit of Tom Waits, preferring instead to compare the group's sound to Frank Zappa. This disagreement pales in significance compared with the interpersonal interaction between Sara and Behrooz, which was facilitated by the revised format of TAMF86. The revised format also gave audience members the opportunity to communicate and debate amongst themselves and with the musicians, something that had previously not been possible on such a large scale.

'Benzin'/'Petrol' © 2008 Gatchpazh, translation by the author

When the sun goes down
Tie your shoelaces.

Lighter and dagger at hand
Show off the chain across your chest.

Call up the one you know
And it will happen in a jiffy
Down here, things are ugly
Legs are up: Holland, Holland

You are awake with eyes closed
Asleep with eyes open

You are your only friend,
A bad influence

Gatchpazh's abstract lyrics are covertly political. Ahmadzadeh told me that the song was inspired by the riots that occurred in Tehran when Ahmadinejad's government rationed gas in 2007: 'It's about a person that comes out of their house and is face to face with a busy city full of smoke' (personal communication, Facebook, 6 June 2009). The Iranian government had warned people for weeks that they were about to begin a petrol-rationing programme, but announced the exact time it would take effect only three hours before. This was a tactical move to stop people from hoarding petrol before the rationing took effect and it caused protesters to set fire to a dozen petrol stations in Tehran.

Gatchpazh's song may sound as random and spontaneous as their attitude to music, but it describes a social and political event that continues to affect Iran's citizens on a daily basis. The version of 'Benzin' that was submitted to TAMF86 was recorded live in one take and the rather chaotic ending attests to it. The song fizzles out to an argument among band members, in Persian, about the song's ending: 'Why did you do that!' 'Just because!' 'Why didn't you play that bit?!' 'Because', and the track quickly cuts. It is this personal and humorous touch that endears the band and Gatchpazh's song to the listener. Never faltering from its roots in E minor, the experiment with improvisatory rock music and jazz is a homage to a style that all of the band's members have been schooled in. Many of Tehran's unofficial rock musicians, in the absence of educational facilities for the music they love, have studied classical and jazz music instead. This has ensured a high calibre of musicianship within the unofficial rock music scene.

Although the band members jam often at parties and informal gatherings Gatchpazh has only performed one semi-official concert so far. Their first ticketed concert was at Sharif University of Technology on 6 May 2009, and their advertisement for the event on Facebook stipulated that only Sharif University students were able to attend. Despite this requirement, friends of the band who were not Sharif University students also reported being able to attend the concert. One week before the scheduled concert, the band posted a comment on the wall of their event page on Facebook saying that the concert had sold out.

Concerts by unofficial bands are a rarity in the Islamic Republic. They occurred more frequently when Khatami was president and musicians were hopeful that if a reformist won the 2009 presidential elections there would be another cultural thaw. When concerts are scheduled they sell out quickly. 127's drummer Yahya told me, 'Back then [during Khatami's presidency] we were doing regular shows . . . and every time we scheduled a concert the time it took for the tickets to sell out diminished . . . it took less than a day for all the tickets to sell out to our last show' (11 July 2008). Demand for concert tickets in Tehran far outweighs supply, irrespective of the genre or musician/band.

Bijan Moosavi

Bijan Moosavi (www.bijanmoosavi.com) is a self-taught experimental musician who studied graphic design at Tehran's Free Islamic University.[3] Moosavi also creates video installations and short experimental films. He recorded and self-produced an album called 'Dar Headphone-ha-yam' ('In My Headphones') and released it through his website in 2008. Moosavi chose the song 'Shahr-e Siah' (English title: 'Dark City') to submit to TAMF86. In the autobiography on his website he writes: 'Childhood knotted my life with music. Azad [Free] Islamic University made me an expert in graphic design. My chaotic society made me an experimentalist'.

Massive Attack, Radiohead, Björk, and Portishead inspired his album. He writes all his lyrics in Persian and he is part of an increasing number of musicians to do so.

In the song summary on his TAMF86 page Bijan wrote, 'Because there is no active musical wave in our country, and because resources are limited, my musical activities remain by nature experimental, experimenting with composition, words and mood'. Although other musicians expressed similar statements in focus group interviews, it is not true that there is no active musical wave in Iran, but because the scene is unofficial and illegal, it is hidden from those who are not privy to it. The secrecy of the scene means that it is difficult for different factions to access each other's work. It is entirely possible that two bands of musicians living near each other and recording similar music could know little or nothing about each other. The scene's lack of centrality and openness, two facets that would foster communication and collaboration among musicians, is one the biggest obstacles musicians face. Because there are very few concerts, musicians seldom gather together to share and comment upon one another's work. The only tools assisting musicians to overcome these obstacles are technological ones.

Pouriya and I became acquainted with Bijan's work after listening to all of the tracks submitted to TAMF86. When I first met with Bijan he had neither a Facebook page nor a Myspace profile and said that he wished to give up on music entirely. We met for the first time on 17 June 2008, at Café Aks, a venue popular with musicians and artists that hides in the basement of one of Tehran's upmarket shopping malls and apartment complexes. Even in a city of more than 11 million people I was never surprised to bump into somebody I knew in Café Aks.[4] The meeting was arranged via email and although I had only seen a caricature that Bijan had drawn of himself, he was instantly recognizable – gangly and pale with a typically handsome Iranian nose and a fairly atypical head of chaotic and curly hair. Bijan was surprised that we had enjoyed his music and confessed that after finishing 'In My Headphones' he had not felt inspired to create another album. Up to that point his music had not been disseminated outside of his close circle of friends. Bijan, a recluse, was very critical of his own work. Pouriya encouraged Bijan to sign up to Myspace, as he had no internet profile. After discovering Myspace for himself Pouriya became one of its most fervent advocates: 'Myspace is literally the coolest thing ever' (personal communication, 12 December 2008). Following Bijan's construction of a Myspace page for his music and a personal Facebook profile and through his work with the First International Roaming Biennial of Tehran his music and films have reached wider audiences. Bijan's public profile has grown steadily since the submission of his song 'Shahr-e Siah' to TAMF86.

'Shahr-e Siah'/'Dark City' © *2008 Bijan Moosavi, translated by the author*

The day starts with the honking of cars, with the stench of black soot
The sun pours fire over the city, scratching at the bark of trees

The sidewalk takes you with it like a flood, trampling you underfoot
People start to drown each other, fearing the other will do it sooner

Good morning, good morning dark city
Good morning, good morning

Eyes are watching you, waiting for you to step outside your boundary
Ears can hear you in your solitude, they know what you are thinking,
you moron

Good morning, good morning dark city
Good morning, good morning

The city stays outside the window
This small room is my new city

'*Shahr-e Siah*' begins with two bars of unaccompanied sampled drums and
then traffic, construction and voices recorded in Tehran are laid over a loop of
the city's ever-present sirens. These noises embroider the repetitive electric bass
and synthesized strings, which loop a descending and suspended harmonic
progression in A minor. The electric guitar enters in the interlude between
the first two verses with a syncopated melody reminiscent of Radiohead's
'No Surprises' (1997, OK Computer) and re-enters with the interlude theme
played double speed in the chorus after the second verse. The instrumental
passage between the last verse and the outro is filled with a tense and distorted
growling breathing, echoing the tension felt by the narrator as he wakes up to
the chaotic city perpetuating beneath his window each morning.

'*Shahr-e Siah*' is an ode to Tehran that describes the city well. The city's
residents are constantly subjected to a combination of both urban sprawl
and polluted constriction. The smog suffocates, the apartment buildings
impinge upon each other, and the Lego-like architecture disappears into
the imposing mountains that loom over the city. Even in the northernmost suburbs of Tehran on the sloping foothills of the Alborz mountain
range, it is impossible to escape the chaotic construction and traffic noises
that permeate even the quietest of houses from sunrise until well into the
middle of the night. In summer, the centre of the city is unbearable; smog

blackens the skin and nasal cavities as it settles, and the heat is stifling. People, rushing in every direction, share the sidewalks with motorbikes, garbage and random objects. And in the main gathering places of the city, the malls and parks and squares, teams of morals police stationed near their vans watch over the populace, ensuring nobody gets away with an act 'against Islam'. From the appalling pollution ('stench of black soot') and lack of social trust ('people start to drown each other, fearing the other will do it sooner') to the feeling of being watched everywhere you go ('eyes are watching you, waiting for you to step out of your boundary') Bijan's song speaks for those Tehranis who are buckling under the pressure of constant surveillance from both populace and state.

All of the unofficial rock musicians I interviewed said they felt oppressed by public life in Tehran. The lyrics show that for Bijan, Tehran's arid and polluted climate is as suffocating as the people crowding the sidewalk, pushing each other down (mostly metaphorically) in order to reach their own destinations quicker, sometimes at the expense of others. Musicians said in interviews that there was a real phenomenon of wanting to better each other's achievements or to sabotage the achievements of others in the music scene. Unofficial musicians criticize each other's work to compensate for their own insecurities. Arya, a 19-year-old musician said: 'We are, after all, non-professionals. We work hard to get places and sometimes when we get there and see someone else has already beaten us to it, we get jealous' (personal communication via email, 15 February 2009).

Bijan also sings about paranoia in his song. Paranoia is prevalent among scene members and it stems from the multitude of ways in which the state surveys the populace in the public sphere. Some of my Iranian friends were wary of associating with me in public because of the attention it attracted and others were cautious leaving their own homes for fear of being chastised by the police for their hair, their outfits, or simply for being in the wrong place at the wrong time. They are very accustomed to censoring their true selves in public so as not to push the boundaries of what is acceptable, which often leads to reprimand. This regulation of the public sphere severely restricts the opportunities for Tehran's unofficial rock musicians to meet. They spend a lot of time in their rooms, in their own worlds, the only spaces over which they have autonomy. Bijan's concluding lyrics float above the harmony's undertow: 'The city stays outside the window, this small room is my new city'.

Free Keys

The Free Keys (see Figure 11) lived in the affluent upper-northern suburbs of Tehran while I was conducting the research for this book. They have

Figure 11 'Bigly' (bass guitar) and 'Ash' (drums) of the group Free Keys performing at their second illegal concert in *Otagh-e Tamrin*, a converted basement of an apartment in a north-western suburb of Tehran in September 2007 (photograph by author)

since dispersed to India and Turkey, two of the few countries where Iranians can travel without enduring the rigmarole of applying for a visa. Cotton-clad hippy 'Kaddy', his dreadlocks permanently covered with a tri-colour Rastafarian beanie, is the band's guitarist and front man. 'Kaddy' is the bandleader's nickname. It stems from the Persian word *kad khoda* (lit. 'village headman'). Members of the bands that practise in *otagh-e tamrin* (lit. 'the practice room') call him this because his family owns the basement, which is the only communal physical space where they can meet and put on concerts. The basement is their village; Kaddy is their 'headman'.

Kaddy has been producing music in the small practice room in the basement of his parent's house for the last nine years. With his band mates Bigly (bass) and Ash (drums), he writes psychedelic hard rock music, which is influenced by the likes of Tool and Metallica. Bigly was only 17 at the time I was in Iran. He relocated to London two months before his eighteenth birthday in order to evade military service obligations. Iranian males are eligible for a passport before the age of 18 and are free to leave the country up until this point. If they remain in Iran past their eighteenth birthday their passports are revoked and they must complete their military service unless they receive an exemption. Once resident in another country they can spend three months of every year in Iran before surrendering to the military. Some affluent families send their sons overseas before they turn 18 so that they can legally evade their military service obligations and others, depending on the level of corruption within the militaristic structures inside Iran at the time, attempt to buy their way out of it.

Kaddy has spent most of the last nine years literally underground. His parents own an apartment building in a north-western suburb of Tehran and it was here that his dreams of becoming a musician were formed. The basement of the apartment building, decrepit and unoccupied, became his hideout and he built a small, soundproofed room into one of its corners. Like Moosavi's bedroom was to him, Kaddy's basement was his 'new city'. His guitars hung on the wall and his recording equipment was stacked into the corner. His MacBook, a rare commodity in Tehran due to international trade embargos, was treated like royalty. The rest of the basement underwent a dramatic transformation in the summer of 2007 and it is this space that Kaddy and his close associates referred to as *otagh-e tamrin*.

The Free Keys, along with their best friends the Yellow Dogs, worked together solidly over the summer of 2007 to redesign the underground space. They had a flash of inspiration after rediscovering the split-level flooring and realized it would make a perfect stage. They were desperate to perform, whatever the cost. Using their own pocket money to support the renovations, and with physical labour donated by a group of close-knit friends who form the bands' main fan base, they set to work. Upon completion, the basement boasted graffiti-bombed walls, laser and strobe lights, and a makeshift stage with space for two bands to set up side by side.

Free Keys submitted their song 'Dreaming' to TAMF86. Kaddy recorded the song, which features samples, digitized effects and synthesizers in addition to the band's usual line-up. An analysis of the textual and harmonic content follows the presentation of the lyrics.

'Dreaming' © Free Keys 2008

Life is the experience of limited experiences
Life can be expanded by dreaming
Dreaming is my reality!

The essential problem of mankind
[is] to believe he's alive
While he fainted in the waiting room of life

Dreaming is my reality, dreaming is my . . .
Dreaming is my reality, dreaming is my . . .

Beware of your thoughts
Beware of your emotions

> Knowledge of knowledge
> The world builds your life
> But in your dreams you create your life!

Over the course of my research I have discovered that two of the most commonly recurring themes in the texts of unofficial Iranian rock songs are 'waiting' and 'dreaming'. In the lyrics of 'Dreaming' Kaddy expresses that he feels more real in his dream state than in 'reality'. He argues, somewhat fatalistically, that life paths are dictated and pre-determined 'experience[s] of limited experiences', which are constructed by the world around us. Kaddy, the enlightened narrator, feels alive in his dreams where he has autonomy over creating his own reality. His dreams are temporary autonomous zones. In the song, Kaddy observes that although 'mankind' may believe they are alive, they have merely 'fainted in the waiting room of life'. This lyric suggests that Kaddy wants something different from the norm and that he is not happy with the life that was pre-determined for him. Many unofficial rock musicians expressed that they felt unlucky to have been born in 'this' Iran, in other words the 'Islamic Republic'. The contradiction between the love and pride they feel for their country and the disdain they feel for its government is one of the many factors contributing to the overwhelming sense of anxiety that permeates the minds of the young Iranians whom I encountered during the course of my research.

Kaddy's vocal performance is enhanced with a digital processor to make it sound grainy, angrier and deeper, as though he is singing through a megaphone with a flat battery. In an interview he described his first encounter with audio effects:

> The first time I got hold of an electric guitar we hooked it up to the amp and started to play it and wondered why its sound was so strange. I thought that an electric guitar's sound was just supposed to be distorted but then I figured out you had to have a pedal . . . Thankfully I figured out how to get a distorted sound without the pedals [which were not available in Iran at that time and are still difficult to come by]. I'd record it onto the Windows sound recorder, then put that on a tape and turn that up to full volume and re-record it. (Personal communication, 7 July 2008)

The song's harmony is repetitive while also being quite 'Middle Eastern-sounding'. This is an ironic twist of the appropriated appropriating the appropriator as the Free Keys' industrial metal and progressive rock influences often borrow sounds from non-Western music. The Free Keys have inadvertently created a song that 'sounds' quite Persian. 'Dreaming' also shares structural commonalities with Persian classical music. The instruments play faster in pace and higher in pitch during the climactic bridge, mimicking the structure of a vocal part in the last third of a piece of classical Iranian music (see Zonis 1980: 272). While none of the members of Free Keys has received tuition in classical Iranian music, and selected the tonality for the song on a subconscious level, 'Dreaming' is performed mostly in an Iranian mode called *dastgah-e Homayoun*. Transposed to start on C, *dastgah-e Homayoun* ascends the notes C, Db, E, F, G, Ab, Bb, C (Zonis 1980: 271). Houshang, of the band Aluminium MGS agreed with my observation: 'I think that our classical music is quite similar to rock music, and that's why I like both . . . The style of constructing songs is quite similar . . . One instrument starts with improvising on a theme then another instrument picks up on that' (interview, 9 July 2008).

Yellow Dogs

Figure 12 'Obaash', the lead singer and guitarist of the Yellow Dogs, relaxing in Kaysan Studios during a recording session in July 2008 (photograph by author)

'Obaash' (nickname, lit. 'rascal') is a 19-year-old skateboarder who has competed twice in the annual Red Bull skate competition held in the Enghelab Sports Centre. He fronts a Kings of Leon and Interpol inspired band called the Yellow Dogs. Obaash was my skateboarding partner in Tehran. He is part of a group of about 20 boys and the odd tag-along girlfriend that meet at one of northwest Tehran's green spaces to skate, socialize and smoke. The Yellow Dogs, a group of four exceptionally motivated young Iranian men, Zina (drums), Koory (bass), Looloosh (lead guitar), and Obaash, are also privy to the Free Keys' private city. They all refer to each other by their nicknames and these have been preserved in this text. The two bands do everything together. They travel together, play poker together, party and practise music together. The symbiotic relationship between these two bands vividly demonstrates a certain type of group ethos that is a rarity in the unofficial rock music scene.

Obaash, the band's singer and rhythm guitarist, acquired his driver's licence, the rights to his father's car and a much stricter curfew alongside it in the middle of my research year in Tehran. His band practised every afternoon in a purpose-built soundproofed and air-conditioned 3m by 2m studio tacked onto the flat roof of their drummer Zina's apartment building. Their practice room is one of the more unusual spaces that unofficial musicians have appropriated. Bands usually practise in bedrooms or basements, but other unusual practice spaces included a sauna (the Audioflows) and a converted greenhouse (127). The Yellow Dogs' strict practice regime entails two hours of jamming every night. Their rehearsals finish at dusk and the band are usually sitting out on the roof railings having a cigarette and watching the next-door neighbour tend to his carrier pigeons when the evening call to prayer rings out.

The Yellow Dogs met through mutual friends and socialize often with their 'gang' in *Park-e Ghoorbaghe* [lit. 'frog park'], a favourite hangout for skaters and graffiti artists. Koory and Looloosh were part of the original line-up of Hypernova, who are discussed later in this book. The Yellow Dogs submitted their song 'Desert Girl' to TAMF86 as it was the only song that they had recorded at that point. The song's construction is strongly influenced by the new American Rock 'n' Roll bands that they listen to, such as the Strokes, Interpol and the Kings of Leon. The song begins with a distorted bass line in the Aeolian mode starting on Bb and the repetition of the root chord in the verse provides a fundament of noise over which Obaash yelps the lyrics in English.

'Desert Girl' © 2008 Yellow Dogs

Empty pockets, no more food, long way to go, too tired to move
Desert sunshine, shines on my head, I said to myself, 'man you're dead'

Long blonde hair, desert girl,
Come on and rescue me, I've got no place to go
My angel, desert girl,
Come on and I'll wait here until you drive me back home

Feeling between, drunk and stoned, no one to talk, left alone
I'm gonna die, there's no doubt, somebody help, I wanna shout!

The Yellow Dogs must have struggled to submit a non-political song to TAMF86, as most of their songs refer to either drug use (far more descriptively than in the above lyrics) in the unofficial music scene, the oppression they feel at the hands of the state as young reform-minded musicians, or their contested status in society and in the eyes of the law. This song represents the band's musical genre, but not its lyrical style. When I mentioned to Obaash that I was reviewing TAMF86 in my book he blushed and said that 'Desert Girl' was submitted in haste and that the lyrics were 'the worst ever' (personal communication, 1 February 2009). I asked him if he would mind if I had a copy of the lyrics and he emailed me the lyrics to all of his songs, hiding 'Desert Girl' near the bottom, hoping perhaps that I would overlook it. Some of the Yellow Dogs' more political songs are examined in the next chapters, when I begin to discuss identity and expression in unofficial rock music in more depth.

R.
Yellow Dogs are by far the coolest band in Tehran right now. They are one of the few bands who are with the times. I have no doubt in my mind that if they work hard and keep getting better they will certainly achieve great success. The sky is the limit as to how far these guys can go. Best of luck!

SalehZ (translation)
Friends, you are the best band in Tehran. The best.

Presented above are two of the comments that were posted to the Yellow Dogs' TAMF86 page. The authors of these comments are themselves members of the unofficial rock music scene. SalehZ was a member of the now defunct 'Up' band, in which he performed with Shahab from the Audioflows; and R. is 'King Raam', the lead singer of Hypernova, discussed in the subsequent chapters of this book. The comments, both submitted by friends, tell us more about the Yellow Dogs than they do about their music. The band has very few enemies and a large friendship circle, something that certainly works to their advantage in the unofficial rock music scene. They work hard, practising nearly every weekday, and while their natural musicianship may be less than that of other musicians in the scene, their dedication has led them to be very good at what they do.

The first time I went to their practice room they were working on a new song. Their fingers faltered on their fret boards and the drummer kept losing the beat. On a subsequent visit two weeks later they were playing the same song as though they had been playing it for months while the freshness and rawness that characterizes their sound remained intact. Many of Tehran's unofficial rock musicians have had limited musical training, particularly in contemporary music styles. They teach each other how to play and they learn technical aspects and song writing skills from DVD-footage and music videos of their favourite artists. Practice rooms also double as teaching rooms and on one visit to a Yellow Dogs rehearsal I observed a younger skater getting a one-to-one lesson on the ins and outs of distortion from the band's bass player. With very few outlets for official music training in the styles that unofficial musicians enjoy, these young men empower each other and build on the communal knowledge of the scene by teaching new recruits.

Kian

Kian Pourtorab's song 'Revayati az fereshteye marg' (English title: 'A Parable from the Angel of Death') was composed around an idea that inspired him while watching a short film by the same name. Maybe 'inspire' is not the right word, as Kian was not at all impressed by the film: 'It was a bad film just like all the other films by our "talented" youth' (personal communication via email, 10 February 2009). In the recording Hadi Rahmani plays accordion and piano and Kian plays electric guitar and sings. Kian's lyrics are difficult to decipher, as the quality of the recording is low and the pronunciation of the Persian words has been altered so much to fit with the rhythm of the music that it loses its natural gait in some sections. One of the biggest challenges facing Tehran's unofficial musicians is producing work with high production values. They often work alone, recording with amateur or outdated equipment. Although studio time in Tehran is comparatively cheap, it is still cost-prohibitive for self-funded unofficial artists. An hour with a producer in a small independent studio costs musicians the equivalent of 20USD an hour. Kian's unassuming song is cleverly arranged and its final breakdown, a repetition of the line 'but I think only of being with you', over the chord progression Bdim, F, Dm, C, is tender. The fact that the lyrics are very hard to decipher, even for native Persian speakers, detracts from the overall quality and listenability of the song. Pouriya and I listened to the song on repeat trying to work out the lyrics before Kian finally posted them on the comments section of his TehranAvenue Music Festival submission page after being requested to do so by other listeners.

'A Parable from the Angel of Death' © 2008 Kian Pourtorab, translated by the author

Today or tomorrow,
Your turn will come
It's not my fault or yours

Someone leaves, someone arrives, and we start all over again
Someone leaves, someone arrives, and we start all over again

It's up to me to take you away from here
My regret comes from solitude
And your fear is from things you can't see
It's not my fault or yours

Someone leaves, someone arrives, and we start all over again
But I think only of being with you

Kian's song lyrics are apolitical and penned in Persian. The stripped-down timbre leaves little for the Ministry of Culture and Islamic Guidance to object to and Kian perhaps did this intentionally, as he applied to them for permission to release his music in the public domain. Kian's slow rock ballads do not contradict the policies of the Council of Music and they have approved similar acts before. His music is non-controversial because it is uncluttered, simple and slow. Kian told me that he dislikes the music of his contemporaries in Iran, deeming it contrived (email communication, 11 February 2009). In the same email Kian described the challenges he was facing in order to release his own music into the public domain, officially, in Iran. 'If I was a perfectionist then there is no way my album would ever be released, because you're forced to work with people that you don't believe in to get your work out there.'[5]

Most unofficial musicians stated in interviews that they are not willing to sacrifice their creative control to the system in order to be able to release their work in the public sphere. Kian, on the other hand, has been willing to compromise his artistic control in order to 'break into the mainstream'. In an email, Kian acknowledged that he struggled to accept the critical comments he received from an audience that was unacquainted with his style of music: 'I don't know what there is to say about my music. I really don't like Persian rock and those kinds of bands, and when my album is released there will be a lot of criticism about how you can't understand the lyrics because Iranian people are always against the unfamiliar and this is what's holding us back' (personal communication via email, 11 February 2009). Iranian society's apprehension towards the unfamiliar was a common gripe among unofficial rock musicians who were often wary of attempting anything too out of the ordinary.

What's in it for us?

In 2002, the inaugural UMC helped to promote a burgeoning unofficial rock music scene to the outside world and, more importantly, to other musicians within Iran. Prior to the festival's inception, there was no centralized space for bands to share their work. The festival's participants believe that this virtual space has helped them broaden their audience base, as there are few physical spaces for doing so. Ali Azizian, a TAMF86 entrant not included in the case studies above, said he submitted his work to the festival because he felt it was his duty to use the technologies available to him to promote his work (personal communication via Facebook, 5 February 2009). Kian facetiously retorted that he participated because 'there was nowhere else' (personal communication via email, 6 February 2009).

Whatever the reason for participating in the festival, the working relationships that the festival fostered are helping to counteract the gossiping and backstabbing that were once all too prevalent in the scene. Ali further noted: '[The festival] is successful in making musicians hopeful, or at least diminishing their feelings of being ostracized and rejected' (personal communication via Facebook, 5 February 2009).

Websites like TehranAvenue, Facebook and Myspace facilitate a communal feeling, and the shared interest networks that they foster are ideal for targeted promotion. Bands can target groups of prospective listeners by appealing to common interests. Over the last four years the number of bands in the unofficial rock music scene has increased and the variety of styles played has become more diverse. This is due in part to the fact that musicians are now able to communicate more easily with each other. Interpersonal communication is a necessary component for the development of any music scene. When interpersonal communication among musicians is non-existent, whether this is for social, political or technological reasons, the ability for artists to feed off the creativity of their peers, which is a fundamental component for stylistic development, is impaired. The following quotation from Houshang illustrates this:

> Music hasn't evolved much [since the revolution] because there's no competition . . . I don't see the hands of any other guitarists in Tehran and they don't see mine so we can't evolve . . . When there's no competition art doesn't move forward. (9 July 2008)

Pay Mann agreed:

> We never had anything close to us to critique, and so we learnt everything ourselves. You know, you're asking who our teachers were, but in reality teachers didn't exist. (7 July 2008)

Ashkan was also critical of the scene's slow development:

> Let me say this. There are a few important things that allow a musician

to develop and we're just simulating them. Firstly, you need to have musicians around you that are playing the same style. (12 July 2008)

Conclusion

TAMF86, a festival designed for and by Iranian artists, was an outlet, a sounding board for unofficial rock musicians to bounce their creativity off each other and receive constructive responses. The festival evolved alongside Tehran's unofficial music scene over a period of eight years to incorporate the criticisms of participants and of audience members, but its following simultaneously declined. When TehranAvenue's biennial event was the only outlet for Tehran's unofficial rock musicians it had a large amount of web traffic but this popularity has ebbed as more possibilities for production and distribution have become available to musicians. The website created a niche and other websites like www. Zirzamin.se, who now host their own online music showcase, followed. Now musicians create and maintain their own websites and exploit the prevalence of faster internet connections in Iran to promote themselves through social networking sites. Through creating this niche TAMF has effectively made itself redundant. As Arya expressed, 'Now you can make connections with various people in the business all from the comfort of your rehearsal room' (personal communication via email, 15 February 2009).

All of the young Iranian musicians featured in this chapter express themselves in divergent ways using music as a common medium. The lyrics of Bijan Moosavi's '*Shahr-e Siah*' described the desire to escape from the bustling chaos and social rigidity of Tehran. The Free Keys informed us that they can only access their realities in their dreams, and the Yellow Dogs escaped the city on their idealized journey to the desert with a pretty blonde girl. Gatchpazh, Bijan Moosavi and Kian Pourtorab write their lyrics in Persian, speaking directly to their generational peers within Iran, and cleverly appealing to the tastes of non-Iranian audiences who crave the exotic. The Yellow Dogs and the Free Keys sing in English, fumbling slightly at times, targeting non-Iranian audiences, and carving an escape route by developing their international fan base through the internet. These two bands have other ways of informing their non-Iranian audiences that they are Iranian, and these methods will be analysed in the following chapter through a discussion of how bands experiment with 'being Iranian' and what the repercussions of this are. This discussion is continued through the concluding chapters as I examine how the global, the local, and the invention and dissemination of identity through music, text, fashion and visual imagery applies to Tehran's unofficial rock music scene.

Notes

1 Bands can select up to three genres from a scroll down list to describe their style on their Facebook profile. Gatchpazh (spelled this way on their TAMF86 page but 'Gachpaj' on their Facebook page, the former will be used throughout this discussion) selected Indie Rock, Funk and Lo-Fi to describe their sound (see http://www.facebook.com/Gachpaj). A video of the band performing *'Benzin'* at Sharif University in 2009 is available on YouTube at http://www.youtube.com/watch?v=vL_KipWYo-E

2 For insight into the grammatical structure and rhythm of the Persian language see Jones and McMahon 1809: 116–19, which is available for download from Google books. Due to the age of the book its copyright has expired, http://books.google.com/books/download/A_grammar_of_the_Persian_language.pdf?id=0bMUAAAAQAAJ&output=pdf&sig=ACfU3U1hVi_Fxr-Xb6t3LHMYZWiuzuuaeQ).

3 The name of this nationwide academic megalopolis is a little ironic. The Free Islamic University (Persian: *Daneshgah-e Azad-e Eslami*) is a private university franchise that is funded by fee-paying students rather than the government. The university chain's official website is available at http://www.iau.ac.ir/. Translated into English the university's name may mean 'Free Islamic University', but it is not free in any sense of the word. Its fees make entrance impossible for anybody below the middle class and it is not free from the regulations requiring universities to provide an education grounded in Islamic principles. These universities are free in the sense that students are able to select their own majors and degree paths when enrolling, something that is determined by the results of university entrance exams (Persian: *'Konkoor'*) for state universities.

4 The population of Tehran's municipality exceeded 11 million in 2006. See the English version of the website of the municipality of Tehran at http://en.tehran.ir/Default.aspx?tabid=12511, for more details.

5 Kian's band 'Comment' never did receive permission to release the album they recorded at Kook Studio in Tehran. Their debut album *Miram Balatar* (2009) is available online at http://www.commentband.com/fr_music.cfm

CHAPTER SIX

Smoggy + city = dirty rock?

Iran has extremists, for sure. Iran has Scheherazade as well. But first and foremost, Iran has an actual identity, an actual history – and above all, actual people, like me.

(SATRAPI 2006: 23)

Iran's unofficial rock musicians weave personal narratives into their songs. They give their listeners insight into the physical, cultural, political and social components that affect their compositions as they play, perform, record and distribute their music. This chapter establishes the argument that rock music, a global genre, acquires significance as it interacts with a particular environment through the local musicians that play and, even more importantly, *live* it. For these musicians, their music is as much a lifestyle as it is a genre. This chapter examines Tehran's unofficial rock music scene from the perspective of the youth at its centre. Literature about influence, identity, expression and musical significance will be critiqued throughout this chapter and the next, and the multiple ways in which Tehran's unofficial rock musicians construct and perpetuate collective identity will be examined.

In interviews I asked musicians what 'being Iranian' meant to them and in this chapter I critique their responses and then query how different versions of 'Iranian-ness' are experimented with in Tehran's unofficial rock music scene. This theme will be developed throughout the concluding chapters of this book. One of the few directive questions I asked in focus group interviews was, 'What does it mean to "be Iranian"?' Some interviewees felt affronted by the brashness of this pseudo-philosophical question, while others were overeager to attempt their own definitions of 'Iranian-ness'. The ways that musicians experiment with sound and image in order to represent the self is examined in this chapter, which comprises an extended discussion about notions of 'Iranian-ness', as described, depicted and delivered by unofficial rock musicians.

Orchestrations of identity: composing the 'self' in terms of local and global ideas about 'Iranian-ness'

Even though religion and politics feature strongly in their everyday lives, most unofficial musicians spoke apathetically about both during focus group interviews. Tehran's unofficial rock musicians possess both a deep-seated pride in Iran's cultural history and a profound contempt for the country's current socio-economic and political climate. Scene members are young, educated Iranians from economically stable families who do love Iran, its extremities and its contradictions. They take siestas on hot summer afternoons in preparation for their night time social encounters, drink coffee and smoke cigarettes in cafés on trendy avenues, lounge in Tehran's green spaces with their friends, escape the piercing summer sun under the shade of mulberry trees, and ski in the resorts near to Tehran in the winter. They are proud of their country's art, architecture and historical artefacts. As well as sharing this national pride, scene members are also united by their interaction with global youth culture and all of them spend upwards of an hour a day connected to the internet. Shahab, the lead singer of the Audioflows, and Gil, a brooding poet, agreed that it is important for young Iranians to be simultaneously nationalistic and global-minded (interview, 12 September 2006). They stated, 'We are going to have to be global somehow, but we have our own culture, just like everyone else'. When I asked them to describe what makes someone or something 'Iranian', Gil replied, 'Iran makes us Iranian. It's a place; it's soil; it's the feeling, the strange feeling that you feel in your blood' (ibid.).

Interviewees found it difficult to provide a non-convoluted answer when I asked them what it meant to 'be Iranian'. This did not surprise me, as I would struggle to explain to somebody what it means to me to 'be a New Zealander'. I would probably highlight some of the things that New Zealand is famous for (its expansive placid east coast beaches and its wild obsidian coloured west coast beaches, or the All Blacks and Everest-conqueror Sir Edmund Hillary). But that does not explain what it means to be a New Zealander it just highlights a sense of nationalistic pride. Ali, a singer-songwriter, countered my brash question with an eloquent reply: 'Just how am I supposed to explain 30 years of breathing in and out? . . . I can only say that being "Iranian" is different to being Afghani or American' (personal communication via email, 1 February 2009).

I also asked musicians if it was important to them that their audiences realize they are listening to music created by Iranians. Based on her research with unofficial rock musicians from 1999 until 2004, Nooshin argued that musicians seemed impervious to the fact that their chances of success outside Iran were diminished through performing styles of music that were not recognizably 'Iranian', as non-Iranian audiences crave the 'innovative and exotic' (2007: 75; 85). The attitudes of scene members have since changed and the musicians are now beginning to appreciate how playing on their differences can augment their success. Current trends are showing more bands singing in Persian, writing autobiographical lyrics about life in Iran, and altering their visual appearance in order to seem more 'Iranian'.

All but two of the musicians I interviewed stressed that they wanted audiences outside Iran to realize that an Iranian artist had created the music they were listening to. Obaash said, 'It's important. I don't know why, but I want people to know I'm Iranian . . . because the culture and environment that a person grew up in plays a huge role in shaping their music' (personal communication via email, 2 January 2009). One of the main reasons it is important for these musicians to be recognized as Iranian by non-Iranian listeners is because they have realized that their country of origin and the social and political elements of their lives distinguish them from the multitude of other bands outside Iran playing similar sorts of music. They say things like, 'I want them to know that we do what we do even though it's illegal. That's hard evidence that shows our passion for the music' (Arya, personal communication via email, 11 January 2009). Or, 'You know – it's sort of cool to be in our position, because if I was American, I'd just be a normal person, but here I'm really strange and interesting'. (Sia, interview with the author, 12 July 2008). And, 'I like it when people realize that we're an Iranian band, because just being Iranian makes us so different to everyone else [outside Iran]' (Obaash, personal communication via email, 7 February 2009). Even if the music does not 'sound' Iranian, there is an increasing trend to exoticize the self in order to be more commercially successful outside Iran. These issues will be discussed further through the case studies of 127 and Hypernova, which are presented later in the book.

Not all of the musicians shared the opinion highlighted above by Obaash, Sia and Arya, but some who were previously against the idea of playing on their differences have become the most fervent self-exoticizers over the course of this longitudinal study. Ashkan, FONT band's lead bassist and vocalist, was adamant in our first interview that his band should be recognized for their musical talent rather than their country of origin or their controversial history. FONT's first and only (illegal) performance inside Iran took place in a friend's garden in Karaj in August 2007. Police raided the mini-festival, which started in the afternoon and lasted about six hours; more than 200 audience members were detained overnight. The band remained in prison for 21 days.[1] Foreign journalists inundated FONT with requests for interviews after their release and they were far more interested in the band's criminal records than its musical ones. In a focus group interview with Ashkan one year after the concert he said:

> Firstly, they [foreign reporters] are obsessed with the fact that we're Iranian. Then they're impressed that we started this kind of movement and that we showed a bit of bravery, and then they want to know what we're doing now. But nobody asks us about our music: what's our style, what are our thoughts? (12 July 2008)

Ashkan's other group, Take It Easy Hospital, entered the United Kingdom on artist visas in October 2008. They asked me to help them organize a series of concerts and although I knew that they could benefit commercially from emphasizing their history as unofficial Iranian rock musicians who had suffered imprisonment at the hands of the regime, I respected their insistence that this should not be made a feature of their promotion. Obstacles plagued their tour. They arrived at the beginning of a harsh and dreary London winter, unaware that it would be difficult to attract a crowd to their gigs in a city where there are innumerable performances every night. The band performed with very little preparation or self-promotion. A small digital promotional flyer was posted on their Myspace page a week before the gig. Their Myspace page had less than 400 subscribers at the time, only a small percentage of whom were based in London. Their debut show at the Dublin Castle, a Camden Town institution, was marred by their rusty performance. Their audience comprised only a few friends, the members of the other bands that were playing, and a few members of the BBC Persian film crew. Take It Easy Hospital cancelled their last two shows and returned to Iran disillusioned.

In February 2009 Take It Easy Hospital returned to the UK, this time with FONT in tow, to try again. This trip coincided with the Cannes release of Bahman Ghobadi's film *Nobody knows about Persian Cats* (Wild Bunch, 2009), a semi-biographical picture about unofficial rock music in which Ashkan and Negar from Take It Easy Hospital play the lead roles. This time they were far more interested in playing on their differences and when FONT featured in the 'Immigrant Song Contest' run by BBC2's *Newsnight*, which they subsequently won, they emphasized the illegality of their lives in Iran and their time in prison.[2] Bearing in mind that these were the two bands that had insisted during interviews with me in Tehran that their Iranian-ness should not be used as a promotional feature, it was surprising when Take It Easy Hospital recorded their first song in Persian and FONT changed the heading of their Facebook page to read:

> [FONT band] was the first band to play in an open air rock concert in Iran . . . the band made the history in Iran's music history [sic] by managing an underground rock concert with some other bands in Karaj . . . which ended up to a huge rush from Iranian POLICE guards . . . All the band members were sentenced to prison for 21 days.

Little else was mentioned on FONT's Facebook page at the time. There was, however, a photo album, entitled 'underground rock concert in Karaj, Is it Satanist?!', under which the tagline read, 'The first world class Open-Air Concert after Iran's 1979 revolution'. Rhetoric used by the band in their description of the concert during our focus group interview in 2008 implied that the concert was chaotic and scary rather than 'world class'. The band's founding members Ashkan and Pooya, brothers, chastised the audience for acting inappropriately, complaining that some people were head banging to the Indie songs and some were dancing Iranian style to the psychedelic DJs:

> Even at the concert we put on in Karaj . . . where we had selected and invited the best fans, if you looked at the audience there was a complete lack of comprehension . . . The first days after the concert everything was really heated . . . Some people from Iran's music university were saying that we were serving and eating blood in our concert. Some people started a rumour that everyone was nude and we'd put on a sex club . . . Then most people said we were crazy to even attempt such a thing. (FONT band, focus group interview, 12 July 2008)

The way FONT band spoke about themselves during my first interview with them was also intriguing. They labelled themselves trendsetters and claimed that they were the 'first and only true Indie rock band in Iran' (ibid.). This was quite impudent considering that the Yellow Dogs, another indie rock band who have been playing together for about the same length of time as FONT, were recording in the soundstage adjoining our interview space at the time. FONT and Take It Easy Hospital have realized that making themselves different and exotic works to their advantage outside Iran. By using rhetoric such as 'first in Iran' and 'world class' they construct a façade of uniqueness in their promotional material. As will be discussed further in the next chapter, unofficial rock musicians have seen that their commercial success in the West is largely dependent on their ability to emphasize their difference and exaggerate their backstories. Few people, either inside or outside Iran, are aware of Iran's fledgling unofficial rock music scene. Iran, as 'Obaash' summarizes in the following argument, is better known for other things:

When I tell a foreigner that I'm Iranian there are a few things that inevitably come into their minds. The Persian Gulf, a vast and magnificent history, and now: terrorist, camel-herder, Muslim extremist, suicide bomber, flying carpets . . . but those are misconceptions. Everywhere in the world has both good and bad people, and this anti-Iranian propaganda makes everyone around the world think badly about Iranians. But . . . if I was an American in New York, or London, and played rock music with my band, I wouldn't be doing anything very strange. It's much more interesting to hear the story and listen to the music of an Iranian band that plays underground rock in this culture, in these conditions, and in this country. (Personal communication via email, 7 February 2009)

So how do these musicians ensure that their audiences view them or, better yet, hear them as 'Iranian'? As discussed above, unofficial rock musicians, citing two main reasons, have stressed that it is important for them to be recognized as being Iranian. Firstly, they want to be known as Iranian because they believe that the 'exotic factor' enhances their appeal to non-Iranian audiences. Secondly, they believe that their music, if recognized as Iranian, has the potential to quash stereotypes and misconceptions about their country and its inhabitants. Variegated identities are created and expressed in Tehran's unofficial rock music community. The idea that identities are adaptable is very important to the arguments of this book. As Connell and Gibson claim, 'Identities are fluid. They can be constructed and deconstructed at whim and on demand' (2003: 117). As fashions change and as new influences take hold, the face and direction of the unofficial rock music scene also changes. What remains steadfast is the scene's inherent collectivity. Castells argues that collective identities can challenge establishments, both social and political (1997: 2). The collective identity of Tehran's unofficial rock music scene stands up for the community as a whole as it challenges societal norms, governmental policy, and outsider opinion.

The allegiance of scene members to unofficial rock music lends them a collective identity, but each group also fashions themselves in relation to others, which constitutes people outside the scene as well as other groups within the scene. Timothy Taylor's concept of 'self-fashioning', more malleable than 'identity', is befitting of the behaviours of scene members (2007: 120). Self-fashioning is an important concept for understanding the construction of the self in the unofficial rock music scene, as the very role of a rock musician in Iran is intrinsically complicated.

In every society there are certain and specific roles that have accompanying typecasts. Western societies have pre-conceived ideas about what a 'rocker' should look like or how they should act, but in Iran there is no local typecast for the 'rocker'. This is why a great deal of the scene's musical and stylistic influence has been drawn in from the outside.

Identities, according to Connell and Gibson's definition, are not just fluid but are also adaptable. As Smethurst suggests, identities are understood and produced 'with the materials at hand' (2006: 86). Connell and Gibson's and Smethurst's ideas both relate to Taylor's theory of self-fashioning. Tehran's unofficial rock musicians all take cues from outside influences about how to 'act', what clothes to wear, how to do their hair, and what music to listen to, and there is not just one right way to be a rocker in Iran. In fact, each of the bands studied had a very distinctive set of musical influences and fashioned themselves accordingly. Musicians follow each other's cues and turn to a multitude of available sources for inspiration, adopting the aesthetics that they like and disregarding the ones that they dislike, creating in turn a multiplicity of self-fashionings that are acceptable to the collective identity of the scene. While members of the unofficial rock music scene may 'look' different from each other, there are some factors that unify them. The most important of these is their position in relation to the state. The second factor is their positioning against non-scene members. Their collective identity is as much about defining who they are not as it is about defining who they are. As mentioned above, the musicians I spoke with want to be construed as being different. In contrast, the bands that Brent Luvaas (2009) met in Indonesia were delocalizing their sounds in order to be received by audiences as more global. Although it has not always been the case, Iranian bands inject Iran into their music in order to retain and in some cases even invent uniqueness. When I argue that rock music is a global genre that becomes significant in a local context I mean to say that rock, as a genre, should not be perceived as being owned by any particular country or continent.

Tehran's unofficial rock musicians fashion themselves in very particular ways. They structure and restructure their 'selves' in order to feel affirmed by others who do the same and to feel unique and different from those who do not (see Gregg 1991: 45–72). Gregg argues that people construct their 'selves' out of emotionally concentrated concrete symbols (46) and that these symbols, which are all required for self-representation, can be defined as the 'Me', the 'not-Me' and the 'anti-Me' (47). Gregg suggests that in order to know who you are, you must first know who you are not and, in the case of unofficial scenes and oppositionist communities, who or what you are against.

In *The Power of Identity* Castells theorizes similarly about 'legitimizing' identities and 'resistance' identities. Castells' model is particularly helpful in an investigation into Tehran's unofficial rock music scene. Castells describes a state deploying a nationalistic front as it subjects its citizens to propaganda in the hope of maintaining a set of social and moral ideals in explanation of his 'legitimizing' identity (1997: 7). The 'legitimizing' identity in the case of Iran is the Iranian government. Unofficial rock musicians thus embody the resistance identity. Resistance identities are devalued and stigmatized actors that oppose social and political institutions (8). The resistance identity is the most important type of identity construction in society because it leads to the configuration of communities and assists in the construction of 'forms of collective resistance against otherwise unbearable oppression' (9). As well as being anti-authoritarian, simply because the state forces them to be by de-legitimizing them, unofficial rock musicians are also social outcasts, because 'rockers' are not legitimized by general Iranian society.

As discussed previously, most of the musicians I spoke with expressed a desire to represent unofficial Iranian youth culture on a global level, whether physical or virtual, with their music. They also argued that Tehran directly affects the music they produce. Because the music being produced by unofficial Iranian rock musicians draws stylistic influence from global youth culture, the songs they write usually do reference current global trends. If it is important to the musicians, as they argue it is, for their audience to realize that the music they are listening to is by an Iranian artist, what features of the music betray its geographical origin? As language choice is culturally and politically important (Connell and Gibson 2003: 131), the lyrics of a song can help define the social, cultural and geographical origins of an artist. However, as the lyrics of Tehran's unofficial rock music are commonly written in English, it may not be immediately apparent to a listener that they are listening to a song by an Iranian band. If text is subtracted from the equation, what other signifiers of geographical origin are there? The mode or harmony of the piece, the timbre or melody, and the ambience of the track can all contribute to how audiences construe and comprehend geographical origin.

'Environmental determinism'

Environmental determinism is a much-criticized and problematic concept. An environmental determinist believes that physical surroundings and climate determine culture.[3] Early environmental determinists argued that social conditions have little influence on culture and that people are the way they are because of where they live. Recognizing the essentialism inherent in this concept, Harold and Margaret Sprout developed a new model, not without its own problems, that they called 'environmental possibilism' (see Sprout and Sprout 1965). Neither of these theoretical models from cultural geography quite befits a discussion of unofficial rock music in Iran, for the reasons outlined below. Timothy Taylor's more liberal equation, 'music = space + place + time', is a very fitting way of conceiving of Tehran's unofficial rock music in terms of both its environment and its historical and socio-political context (2007: 4–5).

The theory of environmental determinism, in its concrete form, cannot be applied to unofficial rock music. If Tehran does require musicians to play rock music, as some musicians do claim (see below), why is it that a minority enjoy the performance and consumption of this genre, while many more Iranians prefer pop and classical music? Musicians unanimously concurred in interviews that Tehran affected their work, but if Tehran demands rock music, then why doesn't everybody consume it? Ali quite poignantly stated, '[Tehran] makes me, and therefore my music, a little angrier and more depressed. Although I must say there's no guarantee that if I was playing music in another country I'd be any happier!' (personal communication via email, 2 February 2009). With this assertion Ali expressed that he does feel as though living in Tehran affects his music while simultaneously acknowledging that, as he has never experienced living anywhere else, he cannot be sure if things would have been any different if he had grown up in a different environment.

Despite their comparatively wealthy socio-economic standing, very few of the musicians that I spoke with had travelled extensively outside of Iran. Some have travelled as far abroad as Dubai or Istanbul, usually to attend concerts or art exhibitions, but few have travelled further. Sounds and images from outside Iran, mediated by communications technologies such as satellite television and the internet, do influence Tehran's unofficial rock musicians and their work, but it is their immediate and tangible surroundings that leave the strongest imprint. Connell and Gibson contemporized the concept of environmental determinism in their book about popular music, identity and place arguing, 'Popular music is spatial – linked to particular geographical sites, bound up in our everyday perceptions of place, and a part of movements of people, products and cultures across space' (2003: 1). Bennett argues that 'musical meaning' is a phenomenon constructed by social context, and states that it 'must be related to the everyday contexts in which music is heard and collectively responded to' (2000: 51). To restate my own argument here and to follow on from the citations above, rock music is a global genre that acquires its significance as it is lived out in a local context. Tehran's unofficial rock music reflects its socio-political context and relates to the everyday concerns of the scene's members.

I think my influences are the things that are happening in Tehran. Anything. It might have been a yell that a taxi driver just did, or maybe, you know, walking down the street in traffic. (Shahab, personal communication, September 2006)

A person's environment really makes a difference to what kind of music they play. Someone who grows up in a country that is really green and lush is going to write lusher music. And someone who grows up in a city like Tehran, where there's always traffic and noise, well that makes an impact on their music . . . we met a band from the south of Iran recently . . . and they asked us why everyone in Tehran plays rock. *I guess it's just because Tehran is the kind of place that requires you to play rock music.* (Shahab, personal communication, 7 July 2008, emphasis mine)

The same musician made these observations in interviews separated chronologically by nearly two years. In both instances Shahab reinforced the argument instigated by the literature reviewed above that geographical location impinges upon both genre and style. Shahab argues that his influences are local and that Tehran 'requires' him to play rock music. The mention of shared taxi drivers is interesting as their pervasive and deafening shouts provide a natural rhythm that guides the pace of life in the capital city. Tehran's shared taxi drivers park in large loading bays in the city's main squares and shout their destinations at the top of their lungs hoping to attract passengers; the sooner their car is full, the sooner they can depart. The cacophony is ironic considering the English translations of some of the more common destinations. Taxi drivers puncture the air with the cries of, 'Freedom, Freedom, I've got one seat left going to Freedom' (Meidan-e Azadi, 'Freedom Square') or 'Revolution, Revolution, REVOLUTION' (Khiaban-e Enghelab, 'Revolution Street').

Pouriya said that Tehran influenced his music 'the same way Seattle influenced grunge and New Orleans influenced jazz' (personal communication via email, 18 February 2009). 'Bigly' argued that Tehran had the same influence on his music that London had on punk and New York had on gangsta rap (personal communication via email, 15 February 2009). Bigly's and Pouriya's comments prompted me to question whether there may be a definitive sound that could be called the 'Tehran sound'. Is there something stylistic that links all of the unofficial rock musicians and their bands together? One commonality, reflected in the statements above, is that the musicians display a profound awareness of contemporary debates about how environment and geographical location has affected other music scenes. They read music magazines and newspapers online and they compared their own scene with Iceland's equally isolated music scene in interviews.

Thor Skulason, the head of Iceland's largest independent label Thule Records, argues that Iceland's sparse landscape and difficult living conditions contribute directly to the unique sound and style of Icelandic bands and musicians like Sigur Ròs, Mùm and Björk (in Johnston 2002). The 'Icelandic Sound' has become a fashionable way of describing music from a particular location and scene much the same way that the 'Liverpool Sound' was decades earlier (see Cohen 1991). So is there a 'Tehran Sound?' Although Shahab's music is heavily saturated with the influence of Britpop bands like Oasis and classic rock acts like Leonard Cohen, Dire Straits and REM, he argues adamantly that Tehran is his biggest inspiration. Shahab even believes that living in Tehran requires him to play rock music. Whether or not Pouriya,

Bigly and Shahab intrinsically believe that environment affects culture or that culture reflects environment remains open to discussion, as their comments about London's effect on the British punk movement, Seattle's on grunge and New York's on gangsta rap make it very clear that they are all too aware of contemporary debates about music and environment.

The commonly accepted definition of rock music as dirty, hard, loud and distorted and male-dominated does mirror Tehran's social and environmental landscape and its soundscape. In Tehran there are few places to escape from the ever-present chorus of traffic and construction or the stifling stench of smog. Most musicians told me that their introduction to rock music was through death metal, a genre that provided them an outlet for releasing their teenage frustrations. Tehran is a high-pressure environment that offers youth few opportunities to release their resentment in the public sphere. Many turn to drugs claiming, 'We smoke hash because it helps pass the time, what else is there to do?' (name withheld, personal communication, 12 September 2007). Others steep themselves in music and some experiment with both. Scene members are accustomed to living their lives behind closed doors. Obaash, in the following excerpt, reinforces Shahab's statement about the ways in which his environmental and sociopolitical surroundings have shaped his music.

[The environment that we live in] has had a huge influence on our music. We grew up in Tehran after the Islamic Revolution. We grew up with the traffic, the *Basij*, the komiteh [Revolutionary Guard] and the pollution. We experienced every moment of happiness, love, pleasure and fun inside our houses, underneath ceilings, in basements and behind closed doors. Just like how our music making has always been secret. (personal communication, 7 February 2009)

Death metal and progressive rock were among the first genres to become popular with oppositionist youth in Iran after the revolution. During the war against Iraq in the 1980s, when Iran was far more closed off from the rest of the world, cassette tapes were scarce. They were a treasured commodity and were shared secretively among friends who made each other mixtapes of their favourite material. All of the interviewees shared the same early musical influences and I wondered why their tastes were so similar. Pink Floyd, Metallica, and Eloy were all immensely popular in Iran. The ban on music after the revolution made the acquisition of popular and foreign music particularly complicated. Cassettes, the easiest recording format to duplicate and redistribute, were smuggled across the border and duplicated hundreds of times, losing sound quality with every new copy made. Kamran recalled:

Tapes would come from overseas, and we'd listen to them and share them with our friends . . . Back then there were no internal influences .

. . We'd hear for example that there was someone at the end of Resalat Street that had a Paco de Lucia recording and we'd set off in search of it . . . We got it and snuck it home and then called six of our friends to come and sit around and we would listen to it together. (Personal communication, 8 July 2009)

Pouriya asked me once if I had ever heard of a band called Camel. I hadn't and he suggested I ask other unofficial musicians if they knew of the band. I wasn't quite sure what his point was, but he did have one to prove. Pouriya argued, 'There was a system of following the leader here . . . Someone would give some music to someone else who would listen to it and then give it to their friends and so on. And then everyone ended up having heard it' (personal communication, 7 July 2009). Every single respondent that I asked did indeed know the music of Camel, a relatively obscure albeit successful British progressive rock band, and could recite a cache of their lyrics. These musicians grew up listening to the same albums as each other because so few records were available on the black market. The albums that rock musicians were able to access after the revolution provided them their early musical influences. As Kamiar observed above, there were no local predecessors for unofficial rock musicians to emulate.

Because of the influence that foreign records have had on Tehran's unofficial music, the biggest criticism that it receives is that it is derivative. Lavie, Narayan and Rosaldo argue in the introduction to their volume Creativity/Anthropology that available resources make invention possible and that resources are, inevitably, bounded by context. They wrote, 'Creativity emerges from past traditions and moves beyond them . . . when distinct visions and traditions come together, expressive cultural forms often become politically charged' (1993: 5–6). This statement can be applied to the unofficial rock music scene in Tehran. The absence of an internal popular music industry for 21 years after the Iranian Revolution forced musicians to turn to the outside for influence.

Today's Iran is very different and the rate of change in the unofficial music scene is quickening as access to a wider range of music becomes easier. MP3 technology has replaced the humble cassette tape and some bookshops, like Shahr-e Ketab (lit. 'book city'), which has two branches in Tehran, sell a small and non-controversial selection of foreign albums. The range of albums comprises mainly blues, jazz, and instrumental reworkings of golden oldies, but there are also a large number of female vocalists on offer. Sarah Vaughn, Ella Fitzgerald and Billie Holiday proudly displayed in CD racks . . . in the Islamic Republic of Iran, lest we forget.

In finding out about the musicians who were the models for unofficial rock musicians, I was also hoping to discover what makes their music 'Iranian'. Critics of this music query why much of it is sung in English rather than Persian, and ask why it uses standard rock chords and familiar and predictable song structures rather than harmonic material borrowed from Iranian classical or folk traditions. Andy Bennett, following Lavie et al., argues that youth fashion themselves around templates that the global culture industries provide them with (2000: 27). Rock music's significance depends greatly on the local context in which it is produced. A 'global template', rock music does not belong to a particular country, and while Tehran's unofficial rock music may receive criticism for sounding 'too Western', people are seldom critical of European and American bands borrowing 'Eastern' melodic material.

Goehr believes that when people communicate through music they are expressing something particular and unique about themselves as human beings (2002: 1). Connell and Gibson state, 'Musical identities can challenge accepted social norms, configuring reactions to 'mainstream' cultural practices, and asserting new styles' (2003: 16). For Tehran's unofficial rock musicians, the composition and performance of unofficial music allows them to explore and invent a collective identity for themselves that differs from the identities that were previously available to them in Iran, a strictly censored cultural environment. Pam Nilan, through her examination of devout Muslim youth in Indonesia, discovered a sense of self-reflexivity in her research participants that I also found mine to possess innately. She observed that her respondents selected elements of the 'vast shifting landscape of products, preferences and practices which resonate[d] with local contexts', and rejected those elements that did not (2006: 101).

Members of Tehran's unofficial rock scene take elements of global popular culture and blend them with both distinct and subtle Iranian elements. In doing this in an environment where what they are doing is illegal they create a unique genre that is, as Lavie et al. pointed out, 'politically charged'. Tehran's unofficial rock music, which can be viewed as a form of pastiche, means something quite specific to its producers and consumers. Unofficial rock music's significance varies depending on individual contexts of production and consumption, but the most crucial component of this music is that it provides an avenue for the invention and expression of a collective and divergent identity to the youth that produce and consume it.

Conclusion

This chapter has connected some of the things that musicians said in interviews with literature about place and process, identity and influence. Through a debate about the impact of social, cultural and the physical environment on their music, I demonstrated that Tehran's unofficial rock musicians feel as though their surroundings inspire and/or influence them.

The musicians also argued that it was important to them that audiences perceive them and their music as being 'Iranian'. Their responses fuelled a discussion about the impact of space and place on their music, which was intertwined with pertinent literature. They argued that Tehran is one of their biggest influences but their comments were paradoxical. Because they have had very few experiences with other countries, or even people from other countries, Tehran is, in actuality, the only 'real' place that they can draw inspiration from. In addition, if they play rock music because Tehran requires it of them, then why is the scene so small in comparison with the city's vast population? This discussion fostered a debate about whether their music is generally creative or contrived, imitative or inspiring, or all of the above.

Notes

1 The Reuter's press release describing the FONT concert that was raided by police is available at http://www.reuters.com/article/worldNews/idUSL0423282220070804

2 The *Newsnight* footage of FONT performing in the Immigrant Song Contest and being interviewed by a BBC reporter has unfortunately been removed from YouTube.

3 Don Mitchell's book *Cultural geography* (2000) provides an historical overview and critique of environmental determinism.

CHAPTER SEVEN

'I am an original Iranian man': inventing inventive identities in Tehran's unofficial rock music

The previous chapter examined how concepts of place and space impinge upon musical creation and consumption in the Islamic Republic of Iran. In the first section of this chapter I present lyrical examples that further illustrate these arguments. I decided it best to organize the songs according to four of the most prevalent lyrical themes. Some bands and musicians feature more than others in this chapter, as their music provides the most concise and representative examples. The lyrics of 127 and the Yellow Dogs are drawn from heavily, as social comment is a main feature of their work. After the thematic organization of the first section of this chapter I will begin to examine the disarray and disorganization of the scene, and reveal how the musicians' own distorted perspectives of how the scene should function and the obstacles they face on a daily basis are perpetuating repression in some while fostering creativity in others.

It is also important to consider some of the similarities between this community and parallel communities at different points in history. While a comparison has been drawn between Tehran's unofficial rock music scene and Russia's counterculture, the uniqueness of either should not be compromised. Because Iran's unofficial music scenes have seldom been studied it can be of great benefit to examine similar scenes in different geographic locations, but the significance of the specificity of Tehran's unofficial rock will be revealed in this chapter through quotations selected from extensive interviews with the musicians.

Writing the wrongs: challenging stereotypes in stereo surround

This section will describe four themes that pervade the lyrics of Tehran's unofficial rock music: challenging stereotypes, the desire for freedom, waiting and frustration, and religion and society. Scholars agree that lyrics are important reflections of social, cultural and political locations and contexts (see Frith 1988; Connell and Gibson 2003). In Iran, where prose and poetry have been central to society for centuries, lyrics are particularly important to an audience's understanding of musical significance (see Chapter Two). Thomas Cushman found that Russia's unofficial musicians borrowed texts from other authors, especially poets, when composing their lyrics (1995: 52). He also discovered, following on from the discussion in the previous chapter, that the Russian musicians he was working among imitated and reproduced the sounds that were available to them, while also using 'their own language to express their ideas' (53). Similarly, Iranian bands draw on available sounds and style as musical bricoleurs, creating their own unique voices out of the sounds and ideas that are available to them. From where do they draw influence?

Tehran's unofficial rock musicians and their peers are well connected. They speak English or French and consume foreign news and media via satellite television or the internet because internal media are strictly censored. They know what the outside world thinks of their country. In many of their songs, the Yellow Dogs appropriate anti-Iranian stereotypes in order to challenge and hopefully disprove them. The title of one of their songs, 'Koskhol' (lit. 'crazy cunt'), is one of the rudest slang terms in the Persian language.[1] The song opens with the line, 'I am an original man', which is followed by a series of satirical lyrics that pose a serious challenge to stereotypical preconceptions of what an 'original Iranian man' is. In the song the Yellow Dogs employ anti-Iranian stereotypes like 'camel fucker' ('every day I used to fuck nine camels maybe ten') and 'terrorist' ('my daddy was the pilot of an aeroplane, he had a crash in some towers on September 11') in order to contradict them. When Obaash barks the line, 'without my daughter, never!' he is referring to Betty Mahmoody's book *Not Without my Daughter* (1989).

My very first introduction to Iran was through this book, which is a sensationalized story about an American woman who struggles against losing custody of her daughter to her Iranian husband. The family travels to Iran, where the husband decides he wishes to remain. According to Iranian law the daughter now belongs to him and he will not permit her to leave. The story is, in summary, about Betty's escape from Iran with her daughter. It was a compulsory text in my high school. Our teachers drilled into us that we should feel privileged to live in a free country. We did not use the book to learn about the history of the revolution or the struggles Iranians endured during the time of the Iran–Iraq war or about women in Iran. One woman's word (Mahmoody's) was taken as gospel and, like so many other readers of the book our opinions about Iran were shaped forever.

Another band that satirizes anti-Iranian stereotypes in their work is 127. In 'My sweet little terrorist song', a Bob Dylan-esque folk narrative, the band's lead singer and lyricist Sohrab Mohebbi sings, 'I just wanna watch Dylan play live, I won't fly into [the] Pentagon alive'. Mohebbi then quips, 'And if they catch me on a plane from Amsterdam, believe me it's not for a political crime'. Here Mohebbi uses humour to distance himself from the negative stereotype that all Iranians are terrorists and political criminals. He retorts that if they catch him on the way out of Amsterdam it won't be for a crime, he was just there to have a good time. Mohebbi tactfully passes comment on the racial profiling tactics used in airports that has seen 'Muslim-looking' and Middle Eastern people treated differently from others after the events of 11 September 2001. Reed College anthropology professor Paul Silverstein boldly claims, 'Muslims are the new Jews', arguing, 'They're the object of a series of stereotypes, caricatures and fears which are not based on a reality and are independent of a person's experience with Muslims' (in Kuruvila 2006).

127's drummer Yahya said, 'My biggest lifelong wish is that we'd be able to travel easily like a real person can' (interview with the author, 11 July 2008). Yahya and his peers desire freedom. Yahya wants to travel outside a country that will not issue him a passport because he has not completed his military service. He wants to travel with his band to countries that seldom give visas to young musicians because they fear they will seek asylum and not return to their country. The next two themes to be discussed relate strongly to this emotion. Yahya and his peers want to be able to travel the world with ease. Desire for freedom is the foremost theme in the lyrics of Tehran's unofficial rock music; the frustration of waiting, whether it be for a visa verdict or social and political reform, is another.

Most of Tehran's unofficial rock musicians and bands sing at least one song that broaches the topic of freedom and escape. In 'Ozone friendly bag' Pouriya, who records his solo music under the moniker Pooy and His Broken Army, sings, 'Well I'm going down, to the end of the world . . . and I'll go and I'll go and I'll go and I'll never come back'. The Yellow Dogs sing, 'Let's hide, take the ride, go and find a place that you feel safe' in a song simply titled 'My country'. In 127's song 'Salvatore' Mohebbi proclaims, 'These bastards have trapped me with chains and scissors', and FONT implore their audience to 'Fly away' in their song 'Forget the magic'. Pouriya's lyrics tell us he would like to escape to the end of the world and never come back. He has only travelled as far abroad as Dubai, and that was before he turned 18 and had his passport revoked. The Yellow Dogs beseech their audience to find a place that they feel safe because, echoing 127's decree, they are 'trapped' by social, economic, and political forces in Iran. The Yellow Dogs write often about the search for physical and philosophical freedom in their lyrics. In their song '*Nini mamani #2*' (lit. 'mummy's boy #2') Obaash sings, 'I don't wanna die for what I think'. In their song 'Flying carpet' (2008) he sings:

I wish I had a huge flying carpet
With enough space for everyone that I love
I would cut the rope then we would go above
Flying over the battlefields and the big grey cities that we had built
Down there, people stare at the sky for a single dove . . .
We are chasing freedom forever . . .
Furthur is not enough
We're not generous, genius,
Our carpet is better than Ken Kesey's bus.

Obaash wrote this song after being inspired by a documentary movie about Ken Kesey, one of his favourite authors. He read Kesey's *One Flew over the Cuckoo's Nest* in Persian.[2] In an interview about the song, Obaash said that Ken Kesey, the bus that he drove across the US with his Beat Generation-inspired cronies and the acid they consumed was the inspiration for the song (personal communication, 7 February 2009). Obaash was compelled by Kesey's story. Like Kesey, he has his own gang (his band, their brother band the Free Keys, and their skating buddies). Obaash starts 'Flying Carpet' by satirizing one of the Iranian stereotypes he deplored earlier in this chapter. Now, he does wish he had one of those flying carpets, one that was big enough for everybody to escape on together, to rise above the hardships and monotony of daily life. 'Down there, people stare at the sky for a single dove' could be a metaphoric reference to Imam-e Zaman, or the Leader of the Age.[3] Obaash has all of his friends on the carpet with him and they are looking down at the supporters of the regime who are waiting, with their eyes fixated on the sky, for their redeemer, the single dove. Obaash plays with words in the last three lines of the quoted passage. He sings, 'Furthur is not enough . . . our carpet is better than Ken Kesey's bus'. 'Furthur' was the name of Ken Kesey's bus, but this line would be lost on any listener except a particularly quick-witted Kesey fan. In Obaash's song it is as if 'chasing freedom' is a lifestyle; freedom is something that scene members would like, yet are resigned to not receiving.

The concept of freedom was often discussed in our focus group interviews. Sometimes I probed for answers by asking direct questions like, 'What would you do if you were free to do anything?' but most of the groups ended up discussing it on their own terms without being provoked to by me. Some did feel free in the moments of temporary autonomy they grasped away from the state. Shahab said, 'You know, when we meet each other in the afternoons to practise, we feel that we've got a space where we can feel free . . . In spite of all our difficulties we're actually doing something' (10 July 2008). Yahya, who argued that he wanted to be able to travel easily like a real person, would stay in Iran if he were free to do so. Even though he wants to leave now he is unable to, thus epitomizing the ultimate paradoxical irony inherent in the unofficial rock music scene. Freedom is a distant ideal and waiting for it is particularly frustrating. Soheil responded, '[If I were suddenly free] I would do anything or anyone that I wanted to! No, but really, if all the doors were open then nobody would do anything!' (7 July 2008).

127's lethargic dirge '*Azabhaye pambe*' (lit. 'cotton wool castigations') features the hook, '*hastim, ama khasteim*' (we're trying, but we're tiring). This line particularly resonates with 127's keyboardist Sardar who echoed Soheil's comments by saying, 'If we suddenly had freedom, I don't even think I could be bothered doing something out of the ordinary . . . A few years ago I wanted it more. We're scarred now' (11 July 2008). He did laugh when he said it, but there were pangs of truth behind the proclamation, which he attempted to disguise as a throwaway comment while his eyes betrayed the truth. I was conducting an interview with Sardar and Yahya while their band mates were in the US touring *Khal Punk*, their most recent album (discussed in the next chapter). 127, like all other unofficial rock musicians are constantly working against the restrictions of their government, their traditional society, and their ever-pessimistic generational peers.

While some musicians argued that they could not make plans or set goals for the future because the political situation is too volatile to allow them to predict a socio-political forecast for the following day, it seemed to me that the real reason was that they were too scarred and perhaps too scared to keep trying. The political atmosphere in Iran is unpredictable, but there are certain rules that remain the same, however restrictive. Unofficial musicians are adept at working around these rules rather than against them; working against them is tiring and fruitless. The lyrics of 127's song 'Salvatore' provide insight into the stagnancy of the situation: 'Today was shitty, just like yesterday, and tomorrow will just be the same'. In his song 'A handful of lies', Pouriya sings, 'I'm just stuck inside of this machine of everlasting scenes'. In 127's '*Hamash dood bood*' (lit. 'it was all smoke') Mohebbi sings, 'We're baffled in this never-ending limbo'.

The Yellow Dogs also deal with the theme of waiting in '*Nini mamani #2*'. Obaash, who admitted to being a 'mummy's boy' in an interview with CNN, sings the autobiographical opening lines of the song: 'Still sitting in my flat, waiting for a refreshment, fucked up on drugs, like a guy who has smoked hash since [the age of] 16'.[4] 127's 'Salvatore' opens with a similar statement, 'I'm living at my mother's and I ain't got no money, I just turned 27 and it's not so funny, I'm spending all my energy on fighting depression, there's nothing left for any other occupation'. Most scene members live at home with their families and many suffer chronic depression because of a lack of social support, high unemployment rates leading to a feeling of worthlessness, and the feeling of being constantly surveilled by both the state and society. While many demonstrated a desire to move away from the family home, this is a dream that is neither socially nor economically feasible as they are very reliant on their families for support.

Self-confidences: team aesthetic in an 'each to their own society'

High unemployment, astronomical inflation rates (Iran's inflation rate has been double digits for the past two decades) and social pressure to live with the family until marriage make it difficult for Iranian youth who wish to live independently. Share-houses do not exist in Iran. A musician who lived with his brother, mother and father in a two-bedroom apartment encountered a plethora of problems when he tried to find his own apartment. Even though he was earning a good salary as a self-employed music producer, the first obstacle he faced was trying to find a real estate agent or a landlord who would accept him as a tenant. Eventually his father had to front up a hefty deposit and rent the apartment in his own name, because landlords and rental agencies do not accept young, single tenants. One of the other difficulties he encountered was his mother's unwillingness to let him go. Eventually he found an apartment two blocks away from the family home. His mother was placated because she was able to pay daily visits during which she could baulk at the disarray of the flat, nearly always in tatters after the previous night's party, before proceeding to clean it. She would cook extra food at mealtimes and get me to take it to him when I went from her house, where his brother still lived, to his, where we would party. The musician appreciated the help but wanted more independence and he had to push to get it. This example of a typical mother and son relationship reflects common familial dynamics. Mothers play an integral role in the unofficial rock music scene. They are often the ones who facilitate music lessons for their children and they cook meals for their children's band mates and allow rehearsals and gatherings to take place under their roofs without complaining. One mother expressed:

> I didn't want him [my son] to be a musician but what could I do? He begged me for music lessons, so we found a keyboard teacher for him and his brother. I don't understand his music, but I know that it is important to him. I wish there was some way that he could make a career out of this, but in our society it is not possible. He needs to focus on his studies so that he can have a future, a wife, children, and a house of his own. I just want them to be happy. They don't have the freedoms that we did when we were young. I don't need freedom any more, I'm too old, but they need freedom, and we can provide that for them in our house. (Personal communication, 24 February 2008)

Brothers, both metaphorical and literal, work together in the unofficial rock music scene. Many younger brothers said that the listening habits of their older brothers were pivotal in shaping their own first ideas about music. A number of the bands had a set of blood brothers in them. If you live with somebody who plays a musical instrument there is not much point in searching elsewhere, especially in a country where rock musicians are few and far between. In bands like 127 and the Yellow Dogs, which did not include brothers, the same types of relationships were also present. In the interview with CNN Obaash said that he loves his band mates as if they were his own brothers. Some musicians in the unofficial rock scene choose to work alone, like Bijan Moosavi and Pouriya, and some who worked in bands felt as though they undertook most of the responsibilities, thus becoming resentful of their band mates. Observing these different sorts of group dynamics throughout the course of the year I lived in Iran led me to ask unofficial rock musicians why they worked together or alone.

One of the main reasons I began thinking about social dynamics in Tehran's unofficial rock music scene was because in some cases it seemed so crucial to the creation of music and its continued evolution and in others it really worked against it. My research has shown that Iranians tend to work with others, particularly on creative endeavours, only when they perceive benefit for themselves. However, the bands that have received the most international attention and exposure have been the ones most committed to networking with other musicians, both locally and globally. Those who are still recording an EP after three years of talking about it constantly blame others for the slowing down of the process but in that same time frame some bands have recorded two or three albums.

From my experience of trying to organize interviews with musicians in Iran, I know how hard it is to get a group of people together in any one place at a given time. Cohesion is one of the main requirements for the unofficial rock music scene's continued evolution and there are a few factors working against this. Because of the lack of awareness about the work of their contemporaries, Tehran's unofficial rock music scene is totally fragmented. Solo artists are the worst affected. It is exceedingly difficult for them to find musicians working with the same influences as them; if they had the freedom to access this kind of network they would not feel so isolated. Pouriya said he felt as if he were following a different path from other musicians in Iran. He would like to work in a band, but only if he could find the right people (personal communication, 22 February 2009). Finding the right people is the key for Pouriya. When he is recording he prefers to do all the tasks himself because he has full creative control. In addition, Pouriya might be more interested in finding band mates if there were more opportunities to perform. When he can be both himself and his 'broken army', in his bedroom-based recording studio, band mates need not apply. Ali, a singer-songwriter, said that 'the economic and cultural situation' in Iran means that if he works with someone else, nothing ever gets done (personal communication, 1 March 2009). Out of necessity Ali learnt how to do everything himself but he also said that he would share those duties if he could find a suitable candidate.

In focus group interviews bands told me that managers and promoters are the key components missing from Tehran's unofficial music scene. Musicians seldom have the opportunity to perform and they are not in regular contact with the music of others working within the scene. Global media arbitrates the exposure these musicians have to western music and, because of this, unofficial rock musicians have a very distorted perspective of the way that things should work. They perceive it as normal for bands to have roadies, sound engineers, producers and managers supporting them as they play to large crowds. What they do not realize is that the road to commercial success is also hard for western musicians. Nobody starts out with roadies or managers. The answers that musicians gave when I asked what their biggest obstacles and hardships were very surprising.

> The hardest thing is that we have to do everything ourselves . . . After we've dealt with all the stresses of life we want to make music. I think this kills a lot of creativity in people. (Shahab 10 July 2008)
>
> Then there's this other problem. You can do your work and you can release a track, but, you have to do everything yourself . . . I'm the vocalist, the guitarist, I play the bass, I make the video clips, I also have to design the website myself . . . I have to produce our work myself, mix it myself, master it myself, and this takes a lot of my time and makes me slower and not able to work as much. And then I've got a real life besides music and this art thing. In the end, like anyone else, I've got to work at something else and make money. (Pay Mann 7 July 2008)
>
> Here you're forced to do everything yourself. If your lead breaks

you gotta go to Jomhuri Street to get a new one. I don't know . . . if the instruments' settings aren't right you've gotta sit down and fix them yourself . . . set up your own effects . . . (Soheil 7 July 2008)

Because it is nearly impossible to make an income out of unofficial music in Iran, musicians must either succumb to the rules and regulations of the Ministry of Cultural and Islamic Guidance or struggle against them.[5] As amateurs, unofficial rock musicians have to support their passion with tasks that they would rather not be doing. Musicians complained about having to cart their equipment around with them, organize their own transport to and from their practices, and make sure their instruments were functioning correctly, but this is something that amateur bands all over the world are accustomed to. I had assumed that the bands would say that their biggest obstacle was the absence of an official market to perform in. An official music industry for rock would solve some of their other problems by providing avenues for generating income. The three quotations above demonstrate how some unofficial musicians are perpetuating their own repression.

Iran's unofficial rock musicians work in trying conditions. As discussed previously, they can produce their music using home studios and distribute it easily via the internet, but the opportunity for face-to-face interaction with their audience and their contemporaries is very limited. Nooshin observed the same phenomenon during her ongoing research with unofficial musicians and argued that this lack of physical interaction causes musicians to feel as though they are working in a vacuum (2005b: 73). In participant-led focus group interviews the bands discussed their dreams and aspirations freely. Their comments revealed that the bands in Tehran's unofficial rock music scene share a very distorted perspective of how commercial music scenes outside Iran actually work. Musicians indicated a desire to play on big stages at outdoor festivals and commercially release albums of original work without acknowledging that for every one of the bands in the international spotlight there are thousands more still practising in garages, playing to empty venues, and living an existence not dissimilar to their own inside Iran. While their most important dream is to be free to play they believe that a musician's only concern should be with creating. The musicians felt that a legion of managers, producers and promoters should take care of everything over and above the performance of music. This is what they see in the 'vacuum' that Nooshin described. The world's legion of independent bands is as invisible to them as Iran's unofficial rock musicians are to everybody else. Pooya commented:

The biggest issue is that there is no producer or sponsor here to put the money up, to find the place for the concert, to do the rest of the work. It's not the job of the band to go and find a place to perform. You have to put all of your effort into making the music. (8 July 2008)

Most musicians found the chores related to their craft arduous and they seemed unaware of the fact that all independent musicians, no matter where they are based, start off in similar circumstances. The main difference between Iran's unofficial rock musicians and independent musicians outside Iran is that Iran's illegal musicians must conform to social and governmental expectations when they are in public. They can only experiment with alternative identities and invent different realities behind closed doors and in spaces over which they hold temporary autonomy.

One of the most difficult aspects of everyday life for scene members is that Iran's religious and social rules and regulations are fluid and non-specific. The boundaries of what comprises acceptable behaviour can be redrawn overnight. Musicologist Youssefzadeh argues, 'Iran remains the focus of struggles among various socio-religious tendencies, even among the highest authorities of the country' (2004: 132). My research found that the clashes among Iran's ruling powers leads to a lack of clarity about the rules, which translates into an overwhelming sense of anxiety, particularly among unofficial rock musicians. Shahabi states that Iran's oppositionist youth live a secret existence whereby they are 'constantly negotiating with the official version of culture' (2008: 115). The disjuncture between what is publicly acceptable and what goes on in private contributes to the high rate of depression, anxiety and paranoia among Iranian youth. Most scene members spend more time at home than outside with some not leaving the house for days on end unless venturing to someone else's house.

Through their incessant complaints they make everyday tasks far more difficult to execute. As it is, everyday tasks are notoriously difficult to execute in Iran and bureaucracy seems to have its own meaning in Iranian institutions. If you need anything accomplished it will take a very long time unless you know somebody who can throw around some weight for you. This is the main reason why musicians want managers, because they feel as though it is a waste of time to fulfil the organizational components of being a musician in their own time. The musicians quoted above use the obstacles they face as an excuse for stifling their creativity, spending their time perpetuating their repression rather than finding small openings in the rigorous state system to exploit. The few bands that have not succumbed to this cycle of self-perpetuated repression have been the most successful in terms of performing local and international concerts, recording albums and building local and international connections and reputations. The bands discussed below are quite the opposite of the ones mentioned above; they argue that these very same obstacles ignite their creativity rather than hindering it.

There is a group of bands working in Tehran that demonstrated remarkable interpersonal working relationships. The Yellow Dogs, the Free Keys, and 127 are among them. They are young men who treasure each other's friendship and follow unspoken codes and regulations that monitor their behaviour. The Yellow Dogs and the Free Keys meet frequently to socialize and jam in an underground studio that they renovated together. The studio is beneath Kaddy's house, and my introduction to their camaraderie came when I arrived at their studio hoping to interview them as a collective, impatient as ever to get started. Kaddy had not yet arrived and as the other musicians were too polite to tell me that I had to wait for him before speaking with anyone, they tried to keep me occupied. As I was setting up the recording equipment for the interview they came up one by one to share an anecdote or chat with me. While I was adjusting the final settings on the sound recorder, Obaash came over to me and said, 'I'm sorry Bronwen, it's part of our group ideology that we don't do anything without everyone here. They're not coming in because they're waiting for Kaddy . . . It's the system of our community' (6 July 2008). Obaash's eloquence as he described their community's unwritten rules endeared them to me immediately. Kaddy arrived an hour late and suggested we move into another part of the studio where it would be cooler and there would be less ambient noise. I complied immediately and dismantled the interview recording equipment. After hastily setting up in the new location (see Figure 13), we began our discussion.

Figure 13 Left to right: 'Obaash', 'Ash', 'Koory' and 'Kaddy' (with a fat ginger cat) during a focus group interview in *Otagh-e Tamrin* ('The Practice Room')

The Yellow Dogs and Free Keys said that they liked to play music with other people because it was more fun. They like their music to have the influence of as many different characters as possible. 'Bigly' of the Free Keys said, 'I like a "busy" music, with loads of instruments all playing different melodies and rhythms, and all of these blend and create a magical sound that no solo musician can make'. Obaash said, 'Playing live has like this chemical effect . . . There is a bunch of people standing there and you and your band put this sound out there for them and the more they enjoy it the more you enjoy yourself'. During the year I was researching in Tehran I heard about only four unofficial concerts: the one in Karaj, which was raided by police, one held at the Brazilian Embassy for 127 (discussed in the next chapter), and two that were held by the Free Keys and the Yellow Dogs in their converted basement.

Another thing that sets groups like 127, Free Keys and the Yellow Dogs apart from a majority of the musicians that I interviewed, was that they did not talk badly about other groups behind their backs. I found it surprising how many people talked openly and strongly about their dislike for other people's music in our interviews, even when they knew that I would be speaking with the group in question the following day. Even more surprising was that they all acknowledged that *khaleh zanak* (lit. 'gossiping') is one of the scene's major pitfalls. *Khaleh zanak* is pervasive in Iran. People are really involved in each other's business, without invitation. Neighbours keep tabs on each other, monitoring who comes home when and who goes out where, colleagues create scandals about their workmates or criticize their work ethic (or lack of), and people fall in and out of friendship with each other easily.

Khaleh zanak: the scene is cutting off its nose to spite its face

Maral, a pint-sized female singer who fronts the band the Plastic Wave and is a former member of Iran's National Video Gaming team, supported this statement in an interview saying, 'In Iran, teamwork doesn't mean anything, not in the workplace, and not in sports' (interview, 3 July 2008). There is a real culture of *khaleh zanak* in the unofficial music scene, which, as mentioned previously, is mainly due to the fear of the unknown. Iranians maintain a wide network of acquaintances and rely heavily on their extended families for social support. This is necessary in a society where you never know if you can trust even your nearest neighbour. In spite of this, unofficial musicians always seemed to complain about having to do things themselves, which may be because their craft, unlike painting and film-making for example, is not considered to be a serious endeavour by general Iranian society.

Argheyd suggests that Iran's cyclical history [invasion, war, resistance, invasion, war, revolution, resistance] has created widespread social insecurity on a personal and general level (1978). He was writing before Iran's history repeated itself once again with a revolution (1979) and war (with Iraq 1980–1988), yet his words still resonate. Maral continued,

'Everyone wants to get ahead but they aren't willing to help each other to make it forward together' (personal communication, 3 July 2008). Ali said, 'We can't live together with peace and purity and not be all up in each other's business' (personal communication, 20 January 2009). He continued, 'They [other musicians] take people under the microscope and point out all their imperfections. They want to play the role of professor'. In Iran people criticize each other to get one step further ahead themselves because they feel a sense of fear and danger. In the unofficial music scene it is because there is a feeling that only the first few bands out of the country will be able to make it successfully before the novelty wears off. Bijan Moosavi, in his song 'Shahr-e Siah', presented *khaleh zanak* as one of the city's most undesirable features. He sang, 'People start to drown each other, fearing the other will do it sooner'. In our first meeting at Café Aks Bijan said, 'People are willing to stand on each other's shoulders to get themselves noticed instead of someone else'. To recapitulate Arya's argument, 'We are, after all, non-professionals. We work hard to get places and sometimes when we get there and see someone else has already beaten us to it, we get jealous' (personal communication via email, 15 February 2009).

Pay Mann argued that *khaleh zanak* is a routine part of Iranian culture and is ubiquitous in the art scenes, where success is subjective and often arbitrary. He said that *khaleh zanak* was less prevalent in the younger generation of bands, such as the Yellow Dogs, and was of the opinion that this was a very positive sign for the scene's continued evolution and for the further development of its cohesion (personal communication, 1 July 2008). Gossiping is one of the most frustrating elements of Iranian culture and it is hard not to succumb to it. There is a real social pressure to talk about other people and it does have a social function. Gossiping allows people to define their alliances, exposing which group they belong to by criticizing others, and I was often chastised for whom I was socializing with. The fact that some people in the scene struggle to recognize the talents of others makes it difficult for any real sense of cohesion to develop.

By the scene's very nature musicians have to instigate, facilitate and develop working relationships among themselves; those who deem themselves superior to others find it difficult to consolidate any friendships at all. It is a character trait that is not limited to the music scene and it works against binding the scene together. One producer, who had an international diploma in Pro Tools and one of the first Mac computers in the scene, had such a bad work ethic that he ended up being gossiped about by everyone. He knew how to promote himself but lacked both interpersonal skills and a morally sound work ethic. He plagiarized material from some of the musicians he worked with and did not allow others to access the master copies of recordings he had made of them. In Iran, where word of mouth and hearsay is the strongest form of advertising, his reputation ended up preceding him and he eventually struggled to find partners to work with.

The different social dynamics coexisting in Tehran's unofficial music scene work to bind some factions together and drive others apart. How the musicians talk about their scene and the work of their contemporaries is of utmost importance as it shows the deep factions that are prevalent and what effect paranoia and jealousy is having on the scene. As the scene evolves and younger musicians come to the fore, *khaleh zanak* is diminishing. *Khaleh zanak* really is a double-edged sword. When/where it is present it represses the scene further by perpetuating anti-social behaviour, reinforcing the scene's lack of coherence. If either *khaleh zanak* or the scene's lack of coherence is removed from the equation, then the other will automatically disappear. The main obstacle preventing the further evolution and development of the unofficial rock music scene is the fragmentation of the scene and the anti-social mechanisms at play. The scene seems destined to evolve slowly until unofficial musicians receive the work of their contemporaries in a constructive way.

Conclusion

The personal narratives woven into the fabric of Tehran's unofficial rock music speak to their audiences of fear, frustration, waiting, the desire for freedom and the entrapment of state and society. The lyrical excerpts that were presented in this chapter were structured around some of the main themes that were found to be common to most artists and groups. This enabled conclusions to be drawn about social life for young unofficial musicians in Iran. From the statements they made in interviews it becomes obvious that unofficial musicians have unrealistic expectations of their scene. They need to overcome these and quash *khaleh zanak* if the scene is to evolve cohesively.

In the next chapter, where case studies of two bands that have tried to break into the music market in the US are examined, some of the lyrical themes explored in this chapter will be further developed. Chapter Eight reveals how these two bands have coped with the problems they encountered on their journeys, how their ideas about the importance of success and how to be successful have changed over time, and how they promote themselves by playing on 'being Iranian'. Over the next few chapters I will lead the discussion towards the book's final conclusion, which will examine possible and potential futures for the unofficial rock music scene.

Notes

1 '*Koskhol*', a slang term that has been in use since the 1950s, can have a variety of meanings depending on the context that it is used in. Said from one friend to another it can be a term of endearment: 'You're such a *koskhol*'. It can be used to express awe when somebody commits an act that combines both bravery and insanity, for example, 'Last night s/he skateboarded down the highway holding onto the back of a car, what a *koskhol*!' If someone uses it in contempt then it becomes one of the biggest verbal insults. *Koskhol* can also be used as a derogatory term to refer to somebody who suffers from mental illness.

2 Kesey's *One Flew over the Cuckoo's Nest* became *Divaane az ghafas parid* (lit. 'The lunatic flew from the cage') when it was translated into Persian.

3 Imam-e Zaman, according to Twelver Islam, will return with Jesus on Judgement day and enforce justice all over the world. Ahmadinejad frequently references Imam-e Zaman in his presidential speeches saying that Imam-e Zaman is Iran's true leader and that he is only acting on his behalf. Critics, including prominent reformist clerics, argue that Imam-e Zaman would not stand for poverty and corruption and that Ahmadinejad uses Imam-e Zaman as an excuse to fulfil his own wishes rather than those of the general population.

4 The lead singer of the Yellow Dogs admits to being a mummy's boy (which most Iranian boys are) in 'the yellow dogs CNN interview', http://www.youtube.com/watch?v=Ghbk7zdEkVw

5 An exception to this is the illegal Hip Hop industry, which also functions online. Some entrepreneurs have established websites to showcase tracks from local Hip Hop artists; the catch is that these artists must pay to have their songs featured on the website. In an industry such as this the only beneficiaries are the producers and the promoters.

CHAPTER EIGHT

127 and Hypernova abandon the 'Axis of Evil' for 'The Great Satan'[1]

As the Iranian Revolution unfolded and the Islamic government took power, Iran and the US excommunicated each other from a longstanding and mutual friendship. Inter-governmental feuding continues, yet many middle to upper-class Iranians still idolize the 'American Dream', which is the title of one of the songs examined in this chapter. This chapter investigates why some young Iranians are so desperate to live in the US and what happens after their dreams are realized. Illustrating the complexity of the turbulent relationship between Iran and the US, one scene member stated, 'I would be so angry if the US invaded Iran because I believe we can fight our own battles, but if they do happen to invade I will be the first to run into the street and beg them to take me with them' (Negar, personal communication, 12 April 2008).

During the preliminary research phase, which included a month of fieldwork in Tehran in September 2006, Hypernova and 127 were among the most well known of Tehran's unofficial rock bands. Their reputation meant that they were the original focus for my research but the research plan had to be revised when both groups left the country permanently. Hypernova left Iran for the US at the beginning of 2007 before I arrived in Iran to conduct extended fieldwork and 127 departed at the beginning of 2008, which was halfway through the extended fieldwork phase. My research had initially sought to discover how the scene functioned inside Iran with these two bands at the helm.

After both bands left Iran the research plan evolved and I decided to examine the effect that these two bands have had on the scene, its expansion beyond Iran's borders, and on the rapidly forming third generation of unofficial rock musicians inside Iran. This chapter will examine how the new music of Hypernova and 127, their self-representation and the rhetoric that they use in interviews, acts as a bridge between Iran and the US, which are currently two very disconnected locales in terms of politics and geography. In songs and in interviews the bands speak about leaving Iran, show their connections to Iran and Iranian communities in exile, and respond to their reception by non-Iranian audiences. Both Hypernova and 127 have capitalized upon their histories as struggling Iranian musicians to promote their work to non-Iranian audiences. The clichés and stereotypes that unofficial rock bands play on and sometimes invent or exaggerate are also examined in this chapter. While self-exoticization is not exclusive to Hypernova and 127, their new songs and their trials and tribulations on their journeys to the US provide pertinent and contemporary examples for examination.

Small steps towards a giant leap: tour preparations and problems

Those who aspire to be rock musicians in the Islamic Republic of Iran are forced to live very private lives. Even though being in an illegal band lends Iranian musicians a unique status both inside and outside the country, the kudos that they gain from their bravery comes at a price as they succumb to the pressure of the conditions in which they work. All but one of the bands interviewed during the course of this research expressed a desire to leave Iran yet they all said they would stay if the rules changed and they were allowed to compose, perform and socialize freely.[2]

The instigation of the Islamic Republic of Iran created a unique climate in which social life was forced to retreat behind closed doors in order to exist. Most unofficial musicians would live in Iran if they were able to create without restriction. The following comments were taken from responses to email surveys posted by a 30-year-old musician and producer, a 24-year-old singer/songwriter and an 18-year-old bassist (all male) respectively. They give varied but essentially similar responses to the open-ended question, 'If given the choice where would you live and why?'

I'd prefer to live outside Iran, because living in Iran, especially as a musician, well at least *as a proper musician*, is pretty much impossible.

I'd rather live in Iran, but I'm gonna need to change a few things before being able to, and those things are a bit out of one person's hands. So as long as the circumstances are what they are, I'd wanna live elsewhere.

Whoever is able to get out of Iran and does not is retarded; however, whoever is unable to get out and is depressed by it is also retarded, Iran is a horrible place, but living in Iran is still a lot *better than living in the dream of another country*.

These responses raise three important points. Firstly, you must work within the system in order to be a 'proper musician' in Iran and this involves a great deal of self-censorship and moral and artistic compromise. Secondly, if these musicians were able to produce and perform the kinds of music that they enjoy at home, their reason for wanting to leave Iran would evaporate. And thirdly, there is a common belief that anybody able to leave Iran should do so, but that living 'in the dream of another country', as the third respondent suggested, is also undesirable.

But if most of them want to leave, why are there so many bands still in Iran? There are two important factors working against unofficial musicians leaving. The first is that Iranian males over the age of 18 must complete two years of compulsory military service before becoming eligible for a passport. The second is that even with a passport, getting a visa to visit the US or Europe, where most musicians want to base themselves, is increasingly difficult for Iranians in light of current global politics. Every morning before dawn, queues begin forming outside the international embassies in Tehran's business district. By the time the embassies open their doors the queues snake well around the block. Touts sell places in the queues and the application process is inefficient and overworked. Scene members often discussed which embassies were more likely to give visas in casual conversations. Their observations were based on the experiences of fellow scene members applying for visas and on the relationship between Iran and the country in question at that particular time; the destination country seemed unimportant compared with the opportunity to escape. This escape route is for those who have been issued passports, unlike those who have yet to complete their military service, which is yet another obligation some are desperately trying to evade.

Thomas Cushman's research on counterculture rock music in Russia found that attempts to evade the army, which he described as 'the most horrifying and alienating institution of the official Soviet world', were common practice (1995: 61). One of his research participants avoided conscription by feigning schizoid psychosis (1995: 60). Similarly, urban legends circulate in Iran about young men paying unethical doctors large sums of money to remove enough of their unnecessary internal organs in order to gain a military exemption. Cushman (1995: 22–3) found that the most common method of conscription evasion among his research participants was to enrol in university and this is a tactic deployed by many young Iranians. Not only does studying at tertiary level postpone mandatory conscription in Iran, it also means better working conditions upon conscription. Tertiary graduates are automatically designated a higher ranking in the military. One issue with this is that males only have one chance to pass the university entrance exams and if they fail they must enlist. Some young men, generally considered to be the 'lucky ones', are exempt from joining the army because they are the only sons of older fathers and therefore considered indispensable to the family unit. Others have used their social networks to find a corrupt government agent willing to sell them a false exemption stamp for a large sum of money, usually around 10,000GBP. It is a risky endeavour. 127 and Hypernova have both struggled against mandatory military conscription and the members of 127 have processed their experiences and presented them in the song 'No Jazz in the Army'.

127's drummer Yahya told me that 'No Jazz in the Army' is his favourite 127 song because it is his biography (personal communication, 2 July 2009). In Cushman's Soviet Russia, there was a military band that would play for dances (1995: 22–3) but in 127's Islamic Republic of Iran, the military follows a very conservative interpretation of Islam in which music for pleasure and entertainment is strictly prohibited. There is most definitely no jazz in the army. Yahya, who said he only feels truly happy when he is playing music, is desperately evading military service.

Many scene members are 'conscientious objectors' who do not wish to succumb to a system that they have no belief in.[3] Mohebbi's lyrics resonate with the way scene members feel about the prospect of joining the army, where there 'is no sign of jazz, just rules and orders' (127, 'No Jazz in the Army', lines 17–18). He envisages 'a chain of unavoidable circumstance in lieu of improv' and 'nightshifts instead of concert halls' (lines 19–20). In the closing four lines of the song Mohebbi poeticizes the biggest fear of those about to be consigned – that the social hierarchy of the military, with its 'superiors and inferiors', will wipe out individuation by playing their 'song in the key of death' (lines 21–4). Scene members fear conscription because their lifestyles have no place in Iran's military. They are frustrated by 'rules and orders' because their lives comprise a multitude of environments in which they are forced to abide by them: at school, at home, at university, and in the street.

The depressed demeanour of Yahya and 127's keyboardist Sardar pervaded our focus group interview on 11 July 2008. Yahya was not eligible for a temporary permit to leave Iran as he was no longer studying and he was unable to go with the band to the US.[4] Sardar, who managed to leave with 127 on a temporary exit permit after borrowing the 10,000GBP deposit from family and friends, had to return to Tehran at the start of the new university year in order to collect the deposit and return it to those who had donated it. It is easier for Iranian women to leave the country as they are not required to complete military service, but they still face the tough visa application process and require written permission from their father or husband in order to leave. In March 2008, as a group of scene members and I descended back into the Islamic Republic in an elevator after the temporary autonomy of a farewell party held at Mohebbi's house for 127, one of their closest male friends burst into tears. As I attempted to console him with a hug he said pointedly, 'I'm not sad because they're leaving, I'm sad because I can't go'.

127 met at least three times a week at their practice studio when they were in the same physical location, creating a timeline of temporary autonomies in the confines of the greenhouse that they had renovated and soundproofed. Posters of the band's biggest influences including Bob Dylan and Miles Davis supervised each practice during which the band's six members crammed into the tight musty space alongside amps, a drum set, a large keyboard, and monitoring speakers. When the group became geographically separated in mid-2008, they continued to work by practising together over the phone and by sending new material back and forth over the internet. In early 2009, the band members that had remained in Iran were called to the Ministry of Intelligence for questioning and forced to sign a contract stating that they would not interact with 127 on a musical level in the future. The band had been together for nine years and had to overcome various obstacles in this time, including leaving their drummer behind as they went to the US to promote *Khal Punk*. It would perhaps have been easier for Mohebbi to find another drummer, one who was able to leave Iran with ease, or even another drummer to perform with in the United States, but the bond that the members of 127 have is impenetrable. Yahya verbalized the band's closeness and the isolation he was experiencing commenting:

> I'm not a solo drummer . . . I like to have someone next to me to play with . . . Thank God that Sardar's back here to play music with, but when the others were here we had a routine where we would play two or three times a week together. This gets me down the most. And the fact they're over there getting to play shows without me just kills me. (Focus group, 11 July 2008)

On the contrary, Hypernova changed their line-up in order to be able to travel as a complete band. The band's two founding members 'King Raam' and 'Kami' met at a three-week military camp designed for young men from wealthy and high-ranking families, which, from their description, sounded more like an exotic summer camp than a military regime. When they decided to travel to the US, Raam and Kami replaced Koory and Looloosh, the band's two other founding members, who were unable to leave the country. They opted to recruit new members. Possession of a valid passport was the main requirement for their new band members. Kodi, the youngest member of the new Hypernova, was 17 when the band left Iran. He was eligible for a passport because he had not yet reached the age of conscription. Although the band's new members were all able to leave Iran, Hypernova still encountered obstacles as they planned their escape. As mentioned previously, those who have passports must also acquire a visa for the country they wish to visit. Iran is ranked 87th of 89 countries on the Henley and Partners Global Ranking List of International Visa Restrictions (2008).[5] This list ranks countries according to how many countries their citizens can visit without a pre-approved visa; Iran, tied with Pakistan and Somalia, ranks above only Iraq and Afghanistan.

Like 127, Hypernova was also invited to perform at the 2007 South by Southwest (SXSW) international festival for independent music in Austin, Texas. Because there has not been a US Embassy in Tehran since the 1979 Iranian Revolution, Iranians must first travel to a US Embassy in a neighbouring country such as Turkey or to Dubai to apply for a visa. Hypernova struggled to get their visas, achieving success only after democratic senator Charles Schumer heard about their situation and faxed a letter to the US Embassy in Dubai formally inviting the band to the United States. Smiling, the American Consulate in Dubai told the band, 'You have a very powerful fan in the United States' (in Raisdana 2009). They received their visas without further questioning and left for the US immediately, having already missed their scheduled appearance at the 2007 SXSW festival by a few days. They, along with 127, featured as showcase acts from Iran in the 2008 festival.

The paths that have enabled these two bands to leave Iran and achieve varying degrees of success seem very different, but there are noticeable commonalities that will be discussed in the next part of this chapter through a comparative analysis of the bands' new songs. The first and most important commonality is that their new music bridges the experiences of their old home and those of their new one. The music these bands were creating in Iran at the beginning of their careers, before they had really interacted with global youth culture, differs greatly from the music they began producing when consciously tailoring their work to audiences outside Iran.

Khal Punk vs *Through the Chaos*: a comparative analysis of the musical and lyrical content of 127 and Hypernova's latest recordings

127, a six-piece ensemble comprising Sohrab (vocals and guitar), Yahya (drums), Sardar (keyboard and accordion), Salmak (trombone), Alireza (bass) and Shervin (backing vocals and *setar*[6]) have been playing together since 2001. Yahya was the last member to join the band and was recruited after being introduced to Sohrab at a charity concert for the earthquake victims of Bam in 2004. Hypernova formed in the summer of 2000 and replaced two of their co-founding members Koory and Looloosh (currently playing in the Yellow Dogs) with three new members to form their current five-piece group. Kodi (lead guitar), Pooya (synthesizers and guitar) and Jamshid (bass) joined founding members Raam (singer and bandleader) and Kami (drummer) for Hypernova's US tour. 127's *Khal Punk* (2008) and Hypernova's *Through the Chaos* (2008) are both full-length studio albums. The albums are stylistically very different but they are both semi-autobiographical and socially and politically pertinent. 127's album was written and recorded in Iran and is sung in Persian (except for the last three tracks, which are English-language versions of earlier tracks on the album); Hypernova's album was recorded in the US and is sung in English.

Khal Punk comprises 17 tracks, 16 of which are songs and one of which, 'Introduction to *Khal Punk*' (track 14), is a monologue that was written and recorded by myself with the assistance of the band's trombonist Salmak. The monologue incorporates some of Tehran's traffic noise and attempts to describe what the genre '*khal* punk' might actually be. When pressed to explain the term '*khal* punk', Mohebbi denied all knowledge of where the original idea came from. He proffered two complementary theories. The first is that the prefix *khal*- stems from the word *khaltoor*, which is a slang term most commonly used to describe the style of Iranian pop music that is produced in Iran's diaspora communities and reviled by Iran's unofficial rock musicians (Skype interview with author, 13 August 2009). 127 experimented with this idea in the posters for the US tour of *Khal Punk*. They printed the words '*Khal* Tour' in Persian script, which reads the same as *khaltoor*. 127's style is 'punk', because of the band's strong do-it-yourself work ethic. The band's humour permeates much of their music and imagery and this poster is no exception. The central feature of the poster is a *tombak*, a traditional Iranian drum. Fastened around the base of the drum is a testament to their 'punk' side – a studded dog collar.

I played around with the second and more literal interpretation of *khal* punk in 'Introduction to *Khal* Punk'. In the monologue I ask, 'So what the fuck is *khal* punk anyway?' Translated literally, *khal* means spot, speckle, mole, dot, blot, beauty spot, mottle or freckle. A *khal* is something that lends unique character to a commonplace object. 127 has effectively invented a new genre for this album by piecing together a peculiar melange of pre-existing and available sounds. Their blend of Iranian folk music, jazz, and dirty rock music is somewhat reminiscent of the stylistic inter-mingling of music in the 1970s punk movement. The punk movement also made use of available objects and sounds, creating something entirely new out of them. In the rambling monologue I suggest further, '[*khal* punk] is really just this bunch of motley kids playing a motley style they've created from their motley surroundings – this grey smoggy Lego city [Tehran] with its flat roofs and dapples of colour speckled out randomly'. A shared taxi driver's urgent shout is heard as the monologue draws to its conclusion 'Enghelab [lit. 'revolution'], Enghelab, Enghelab'.

Figure 14 Sohrab Mohebbi (facing forward with the microphone) performing with 127 in their farewell concert on Valentine's Day 2008. The concert was held at the Brazilian Embassy in Tehran where the rules of the Islamic Republic of Iran do not apply. Members of the crowd rushed onto the stage, seizing the rare opportunity to dance as they collectively snatched a moment of temporary autonomy from the state (photograph by author)

In a review of *Khal Punk* for the online magazine *Zirzamin.se*, Nassir Mashkouri calls 127 'one of the most influential and pioneering groups to come out of the unofficial music scene in the last decade' (2009, translated by author). 127 are the scene's most well-known band and their peers lauded the assistance 127 has given other bands in the form of music lessons, the sharing of their practice space and their encouragement. Mashkouri labels the band's style 'Persian avant-garde' and states that *Khal Punk* will have 'a lasting impact [on the scene] and will influence the music of tomorrow's generation of Iranian musicians' (ibid.). Mashkouri argues that the album, by combining sounds borrowed from jazz, *khaltoor*, the refrains of street musicians, punk, alternative music and *roohouzi*, has effectively created 'a modern protest music with an Iranian essence . . . expressing the melancholy of life in inner-city Iran and making fun of the city's inherent contradictions' (ibid.).[7] Roxana Hadadi states '[127's] music has piqued the attention of both Iranians and hipsters alike, with descriptive lyrics that speak of the hardships associated with living in Iran, from the isolation citizens feel from their government . . . to dealing with foreigners thinking you're a terrorist' (2008).

Figure 15 'Raam' relaxing on the couch in the early afternoon after a night of socializing with his band mates and some of their close friends at Hypernova's practice studio in Tehran (17 September 2006, photograph by author)

When Hypernova were in Iran they practised in a dead room built by the band in the basement apartment of Raam's father's apartment complex; in the US they say they like to 'play in dirty, disgusting places to stay underground' (www.hypernova.com). Except for a few stray Tehrani cockroaches, ubiquitous across the city, the basement apartment was not dirty or disgusting, and the lives they led in Tehran were certainly not rife with poverty. In fact, 'King Raam' (see Figure 15) chose his pseudonym due to the fact that he could 'live like a King' in Iran (personal communication, 14 September 2006). *Through the Chaos* is, at present, only available for purchase at the band's live gigs, but six of the album's ten songs can be streamed from their Myspace page (www.myspace.com/hypernova). The band had started recording an unofficial EP while still in Iran called *Who Says You Can't Rock in Iran?* but removed these tracks from their website when it was redesigned to incorporate their new recordings and, more importantly, their new image. NPR (National Public Radio), who interviewed the band shortly after they arrived in the US in 2007, still host two songs from this first EP on their website.[8]

Through the Chaos was recorded in Los Angeles and produced by Austrian-born musician Herwig Maurer. Sean Beavan, renowned for his dark and industrial trademark sound and for his work with the bands No

Doubt, Nine Inch Nails and Marilyn Manson, engineered the album. The cover of *Through the Chaos*, by a Virginia-based illustration and graphic design team called 'Pillowhead', was selected from a number of potential artworks proffered by fans after the band posted a request for submissions on their website. Bryan Kremkau (2008), writing for the music website Readjunk, describes *Through the Chaos* as 'a mixture of dark alternative pop mixed with a thick and sweet melodic dance rock'. Lead singer Raam, in an interview with the same author said, '*Through the Chaos* is basically the story of Hypernova. From the first track to the last, the album tells the story of our lives' (ibid.).

Hypernova's music is reminiscent of the California-based band Queens of the Stone Age, English alternative rock band Arctic Monkeys and the New York band the Strokes who are renowned for reviving garage rock in the formative years of the twenty-first century. While an audience listening to 127's new music from *Khal Punk* immediately senses that they are listening to something Iranian, Hypernova's heavily derivative music, when disentangled from its socio-political context, could easily be misconstrued as another offering from one of New York's many indie rock bands. Both Hypernova and 127 now reside in Brooklyn. Two songs from each band have been selected for comparative analysis in this section. '*Mellat-e Sarfaraz*' (lit. 'the proud nation') and '*Charand Goft*' (lit. 'he spoke nonsense'), the two songs from *Khal Punk* examined in this section, were chosen because 127's fans suggested that these were their favourite tracks in a discussion thread initiated by the band on their Facebook page. Hypernova's Facebook fans agreed that 'American Dream' and 'Viva la Resistance' were their two favourite tracks from *Through the Chaos*.[9]

Rolling triplets on the snare coupled with Mohebbi's rap-like vocal delivery lend overtones of an off-kilter military march to 127's spiralling 6/8 song '*Charand Goft*'. Lyrically, the song is very clever. Mohebbi and I collaborated and devised an appropriate translation for the complex and extended metaphor embedded within the text of the song, which opens with the phrase, 'Let this day be night and then night will be day, it's not the sun but the moon that illuminates midday'. From its opening phrase '*Charand Goft*' scoffs satirically at the contradictions of the Islamic Republic. The chorus illustrates the main theme of the song – which is that even sound advice may fall on deaf ears: 'Whoever said anything except for what I said spoke nonsense; there's no point in reading Yasin [a long chapter from the Quran] to the fool or giving advice to the deaf'. The rest of the song exaggerates the theme of contradictions: 'Halva is not sweet and opium is not bitter . . . the earth is not round and such is not decreed, it's nothing but a conspiracy from that sly, deceitful sect'.[10]

From the words that Mohebbi selects to use in '*Charand Goft*' it is clear that the recipient of his scorn is Iran's religious authorities. Their rhetoric is very specific, comprising oft-uttered phrases, and in their speeches Iran's ayatollahs and religious leaders consistently refer to the West as a deceitful sect and a propagator of conspiracies, whereas Sohrab and his peers believe the opposite. In the final verse of the song Mohebbi expresses his thoughts on youth and religion. His lyrics quip that libertines are the ones who hold integrity and possess the moral high ground, 'Integrity is with libertinism; virtue can be bought'. The idea that virtue can be bought and is not always earned is an important theme in the song and it carries through into the concluding phrase where Mohebbi sings, 'Importance is a well-connected dad; progress is three steps back and one step forward'. This utterance is very indicative of the feeling that politically aware and anti-establishment young Iranians have. First, importance is placed on *whom* you know rather than what you know in a country where centuries of hierarchical rule have ensured a 'well-connected dad' is a very important asset. Secondly, 'progress', as Mohebbi describes it, is not progress at all but a slow retreat. These musicians and their peers are part of a wider movement involved in an ongoing tug of war over social and cultural freedoms with the Iranian authorities.

'Mellat-e Sarfaraz' is a syncopated track in 4/4 that modulates up a half step in the verse while Mohebbi enunciates the lyrics without melody in a rap-like delivery style. This modulation lends a sense of urgency to the text, which is eventually released by a melodic chorus where layers of backing vocals harmonize the main tune. As with all of the songs on the album, the chorus lyrics are intentionally simple and rhythmic, creating juxtaposition with the lyrical complexity of the verses. Whenever the album was played at parties a furore ensued with each chorus as the partygoers joined forces to sing these anthemic phrases.

Mohebbi reappropriates the terminology of the theocracy in 'Mellat-e Sarfaraz' in order to criticize it. Mohebbi explained that his use of the term 'mellat' was intended to satirize Khomeini's use of the term (Skype interview with author, 13 August 2009). At the time of the Iranian Revolution, and indeed in the years following, Khomeini separated Iranians into 'mellat' (lit. 'the nation') and 'omat' (lit. 'the believers/followers'). Khomeini believed that the nation should subsume to religiosity and anything he deemed to be nationalistic or against the regime's ideals were outlawed in the formative years of the Islamic Republic.[11] In 'Mellat-e Sarfaraz' the regime is described as, 'Committing treason against friends [in order to] protect the enemy'. Iran's strategic support of Lebanon's Hezbollah, who possess the strategic access to Israel that Iran needs, seemingly takes priority over the protection of Iran's own peoples.[12] While millions of Iranians live beneath the breadline struggling to survive, Iran's authorities organize and televise elaborate marches in support of the Palestinian cause and spend large sums of money on the manufacture of elaborate banners, which adorn the central lamp-post pillars on highways. The authorities entice 'supporters' to these marches from Iran's rural areas by promising a free bus ride to and from the city and a free lunch. The placards they hold and the t-shirts they wear are mass-produced by the government.

Mohebbi, recognizing the plight of poorer Iranians sings, 'Get your share quickly and bow your head, if you've used up your coupons there's no other way, put your tail between your legs if you've got any sense'. Iranians are entitled to support from the government in the form of coupons, which are valid for staple foods like rice and flour. On coupon issue day, the queues of people collecting their rations are long. Mohebbi uses this metaphor to show one of the many ways in which the system dominates the lives of Iranian people. 127's album, recorded in Iran, is mainly addressing their generational peers within the country. The inclusion of three English-language re-workings as bonus tracks is an indication of how the band is attempting to tailor their new music, a very Iranian style, to a non-Iranian audience. Hypernova's album is stylistically different because *Through the Chaos* was designed to tell their story to an 'outside' audience comprising both non-Iranians and Iranian youth born in diaspora, neither of whom is necessarily familiar with Iranian culture and every day life.

Josh Henaman (2008) describes the song 'American Dream' as 'a gut punch of reality to anyone with even a bit of knowledge of the band's past' in a review of a Hypernova concert for the online magazine *Mishmash*. On first listen the song comes across like any other pop/rock tune; the simple chord structure nods to the Beatles and the band's other Brit Pop influences with its jangling guitars. Lyrically, 'American Dream' describes an important issue for the band. The song begins, 'I know that I'll never go back home, to the life I had, the life that I had known'. At the beginning of their tour, one of their biggest fears was to be seen criticizing the Iranian government from the US, an act that would have ruined their chances of being able to go back to Iran.

From the outset, Raam battled with reporters who were more interested in getting a controversial quotation to boost the impact of their news story than in the music the band was producing. In 'American Dream' Raam sings in response, 'They tell me to dress so to scare, look so tough like you just don't care, we'll package you and put you on display, and everyone gets a car'. Hypernova, like other Iranian bands, is all too aware that part of their main appeal is the fact that they are from Iran. In Iran the establishment controls the type of music Hypernova plays by banning it; in the US the establishment controls the type of music Hypernova plays, and also how they present it, by enticing the band to broaden their appeal by playing on their backstory. Raam, raised partly in the US, has a keen understanding of the way the media and music industry works and he has self-styled himself to be a cultural ambassador for his generational peers in Iran.

As time has progressed and the band has become more widely known, partly through touring across the US with the UK band Sisters of Mercy, Raam has opened up more to reporters. Both his old and new rhetoric as Hypernova's leader and spokesman will be closely examined in the next section. Raam's new frame of mind stems from the fact that he feels more secure in his current situation. In the beginning, concerned that the hype surrounding them would die out, he spoke carefully and tentatively about the country's politics in interviews. Now that the band has a steady gigging schedule and a steadily increasing fan base, Raam feels able to speak more freely, although his closing statement in the song does acknowledge the temporary nature of his current situation: 'Nobody grows old in Hollywood'.

'American Dream' is a semi-autobiographical tale describing life as an Iranian musician in diaspora, trying to succeed in the midst of Hollywood's well-established entertainment industry, which is where the band recorded their album. The song 'Viva la Resistance' describes their lives as young anti-regime musicians in Iran. It addresses the band's generational peers, encouraging young girls and boys to keep shouting and dancing, 'Because it ain't no fucking crime'. The song's driving chorus, sums up the band's ideology (one that differs markedly from that of Iran's ruling regime) as Raam sings, 'I will not bow down to your god, this is not who I am, I will not give in to your lies'. The perceived lies and contradictions of the Iranian government are themes that both 127 and Hypernova have attacked in different ways with their new music. Raam sings, 'Your theocratic neo-fascist ideology is getting in the way of my biology'. He continues, 'The book says no, but my body wants more'. These phrases summarize how the band felt in Iran, battling against strict religiosity as they desired to take part in what they perceive to be a normal part of global youth culture: dancing, singing and playing music.

Again, alluding to the temporary nature of Hypernova's current circumstance, Raam sings, 'I know that you only wanna feel everything you only felt while in your dreams, so dance like you've never danced, scream like you've never screamed, 'cause this one might be your last'. With this phrase Hypernova call on their contemporaries to enjoy their temporary moments of freedom. The phrase also recognizes the fact that performing to crowds, being able to move freely on stage, being able to record the type of music the band enjoys, were all just dreams in the Islamic Republic. Importantly, at the end of the song, Raam acknowledges the ramifications that his outspokenness may have on his ability to return to Iran, insinuating, in the same breath, that he is no longer concerned: 'Oh you can burn down my house, throw me for life, take what you want, do what you like, but you'll never succeed. I'm breaking my heart, I'm breaking my soul, I've reached a point where I just don't care no more'. One of the ways that bands and their audiences become empowered is through the construction of collective identities and this will be discussed further in the next section through an examination of the bands' new images and how they have chosen to present them.

Composing clichés: playing on being Iranian for commercial gain

Part of what makes 127's Iranian-ness instantly recognizable in the songs from *Khal Punk* is that they sing in Persian, but this has not always been the case. Nooshin (2005b: 483) quotes extensively from an interview TehranAvenue reporter Hesam Garshasbi conducted with 127, in which the band stated, '[We sing in English] because that's the language of rock music . . . We have to become universal . . . We can also express our local concerns through the lyrics but that doesn't mean we'd have to change the language'. At the beginning of 127's career the question that all reporters asked them was 'Why do you sing in English?' The band tired of it very quickly. They felt they should not have to justify their choice to sing in English, when 'German Rock is never sung in German, and if it is, it will never go beyond German borders' (ibid.). Nooshin, discussing 127 at the International Society for Iranian Studies Conference, argued that the band would be more successful outside Iran if they 'sounded more Iranian' (2006). However the band, who had performed at SXSW, appeared in films and television shows in Europe and had been interviewed by international media, already seemed quite successful, especially considering the number of bands vying for those opportunities. Nooshin's argument that 127 would appeal more to non-Iranian audiences and also to diasporic Iranians nostalgic for the sounds (however imagined) of home if they were to play on their Iranian-ness in future work, proved prophetic, as this is what they have done with *Khal Punk*.

An important paradox of Iran's unofficial rock music scene is this: while bands dream of breaking out of Iran, being embraced by global youth culture and accepted as 'musicians', the content or substance of their music actually has very little bearing on their appeal to audiences outside Iran. It is not only 127 that has been disquieted by the line of questioning that most non-Iranian reporters interviewing unofficial Iranian bands take. When I interviewed FONT, their lead singer Ash told me, 'Nobody asks us about our style, our influences, our thoughts . . . They just go crazy over the fact that we are from Iran and that we are rockers in "Ahmadinejad's country". That's got nothing to do with us, how about our music?!' (12 July 2008). This is the same band that said they wanted their musical records to be famous, not their criminal records. However, as mentioned previously, when FONT came to the UK to perform they realized that it was of benefit to emphasize the latter. This phenomenon, where the political context plays a larger role in ensuring intrigue than musical content, is not unique to Iran. Mitchell discovered that early 1990s Czech rock, which had low production values due to the limited technology available to musicians, was only compelling to those outsiders who were interested in the political context that the music was created in (1992: 201). In the case of Iran, a 23-year-old musician said poignantly:

> Right now, we are getting very interesting to outsiders . . . because Iranian Rock is offering something in contrast with what the politics shows . . . but I don't think this is going to last forever . . . [Outsiders are interested] because, they feel like there are things that we see but they don't. But, after a while, they will surely get to know things that they see but WE don't – which makes us just regulars again. (Personal communication, 2 January 2007)

The self-reflexivity this quotation exemplifies is characteristic of Iran's unofficial rock musicians. They are, as has been expressed many times in this book, all too aware that what makes them special is not so much the music they play as how, why and where they play it. Some musicians, while acknowledging this, may wish it were not the case, but many of the bands have started to play on their difference. They have come to the conclusion that it is the quickest way to garner attention. Recognizing that being Iranian makes them 'special' and intriguing to outsiders drives these bands, consciously or subconsciously, to create an aura of exoticism around themselves. As previously outlined in this chapter, Hypernova has especially struggled with what to say about their politics and legally contested status in interviews but, interestingly, their rhetoric has changed over time. This occurred when they began to feel more secure in the US. Hypernova's story is much more interesting to the western media than their music, and all of the journalistic reports on the band so far have focused on the fact that what these bands do is 'highly' illegal in Iran, going so far as to exaggerate the truth.

In an interview with NPR at the beginning of their tour of the US, Raam stated the truth: 'There's an element of danger involved in what we do. But the laws are so chaotic back home that they're hardly enforced. Ninety-nine out of one hundred times you can easily get away with anything' (in Meraji 2007). The reality is that Iran's penal code prescribes 80 lashes for a Muslim found intoxicated (Book 4, Part 6, Article 174) and between three months to a year in prison, a hefty fine, and up to 74 lashes for 'anyone who publicizes any picture, text, photograph, drawing, article, newsletter, newspaper, movie, or *any other thing that violates public morals*' (Book 5, Chapter 18, Article 640, emphasis mine). But nearly all instances of illicit behaviour go unnoticed and thereby unpunished.[13] Raam's biggest concern was that he would say something in published interviews that could be construed as being against the Iranian government, a crime that can see the perpetrator imprisoned for six months to two years (Book 5, Chapter 2, Article 514). Voicing this fear Raam said, 'We sort of have to stay on top of our game and make sure that . . . journalists don't take too much advantage

. . . because it's our lives on the line, not theirs . . . they can get their story, but we want our lives back' (in Meraji 2007).

Hypernova continued to speak cautiously about their music and their lives, giving reporters just enough to make a good story but refraining from ideological quotations, until after the conclusion of their tour with the Sisters of Mercy in the summer of 2009. And then, in an interview with Freya Petersen (18 June 2009) following the tour's conclusion and a few days after the result of the controversial 2009 Iranian presidential elections was announced, Raam spoke for the first time with quite reckless abandon: 'The oppressive government is continuously trying to clean up after itself through misinformation and propaganda . . . There have been many other fascists . . . who have suppressed the people and the truth far too long before they were defeated, but thanks to the amazing flow of information there is only so much that this fascist government can do'. In an interview with the same reporter two years prior Raam had said, 'We're on a cultural mission, we're not here to make political statements. We came here with a message of unity' (Petersen 2007). Recognizing that the success of the band has helped reassure them, Petersen stated in a follow-up story, 'With their growing success, Raam now feels confident in using the band's profile to promote the causes of democracy and freedom in his home country' (2009).

And even when reporters attempt to steer away from highlighting difference they end up inadvertently solidifying it. Josh Henaman (2008), a music reviewer, boldly claimed in the opening of his piece, 'Hypernova is not an Iranian band'. The intention behind his statement was to make sure his review would be about their music rather than the context that it was produced in, but his words had the opposite effect; the history is simply too intriguing for reporters to leave out. Henaman writes, 'We're pretty sure the band members themselves are . . . tired of seeing it reiterated . . . headline after headline . . . [but] try honing your craft under a regime where the threat of arrest and physical harm for even humming a hook from Western music was a distinct possibility' (ibid.). So much for Henaman's attempt to steer clear of stereotypes. In Iran, contrary to this statement, you will not be arrested walking down the street humming a western tune. Young Iranians stride past the police in time with western beats thumping from their MP3 players and while this may have been problematic ten years ago, it barely registers on their radar today. By sensationalizing the potential for punishment Henaman also plays on Hypernova's difference and traps the reader in a perpetuating cycle of simultaneous pity and wonderment for the Iranian bands.

MTV headlined their report on the band 'Meet Iran's Hypernova: a rock band from a country that arrests rock bands' (Kaufman 2007); Meraji's (2007) headline put it simply, 'Hypernova: Illegal indie-rock from Iran'. Hypernova, like other bands, use their difference to promote themselves quite calculatedly. They wrote in 'Our Story' on their Myspace page, 'Iran may not seem the most likely breeding ground for young up-and-coming musicians but, thanks to a few daring pioneers, doors that were seemingly locked tight by the strict moral laws have been cracked'. Although some of their messages are similar, both Hypernova and 127 have chosen to present their new music in different ways. So, how do their audiences receive them?

Electronic audiences

Researchers interested in audience reception typically analyse audience responses by attending concerts in order to survey the atmosphere and to interview audience members or by interviewing audiences away from the concert context. In the case of this book, a majority of the audience consumes the music electronically because the opportunity to attend concerts by unofficial musicians is so limited. I have surveyed audience responses to Hypernova and 127 through the internet, a medium that crosses both geographic and political boundaries. When a group like Hypernova or 127 perform in a club in New York City only a select number of people, usually locals who have pre-purchased tickets, can access the music. When these bands publish a new recording or a video of a performance on their Myspace page or Facebook profile anyone with an internet connection, whether inside Iran using an anti-filter or outside Iran, can access it. More importantly, electronic audiences are able to interact with the music by commenting on it through the techno-logical facilities of these social networking sites. Below is a survey of some of the comments posted to 127's and Hypernova's Myspace pages and Facebook profiles during the course of their time in the US. Some of the comments were posted by Iranians living in Iran, some by Iranians in diaspora, but non-Iranian audience members who have heard about the bands through the media or word of mouth have posted a majority of the comments.

When Hypernova relaunched their Myspace page on 28 October 2007 they had just finished recording the first songs for their new album in the US. They removed all of the old material from their page, including roughly recorded demo songs, comments posted by fans and photographs of the band wearing their trademark mismatched and brightly coloured clothes in Tehran. Suddenly, as they slung their new image into orbit, the bright hooded sweatshirts, vintage suit jackets and straight-legged jeans that characterized Hypernova's look while they were in Iran were gone. Their new look was much darker: tailored suits, pencil ties and beards. They collected a legion of fans as they toured the US on two separate occasions, first with IAMX and then with the Sisters of Mercy.

Hypernova has three distinct target audiences: Iranians in diaspora, young Iranians inside Iran and non-Iranian youth. For youth born to Iranian parents in diaspora, the band provides a point of connection with a homeland they may never have visited. Hypernova gives these youth something to show to those who have fallen for the media's portrayal of Iran as dark and fearful. Two comments stood out as I sifted through the dozens of pages of Hypernova's Myspace comments. The first was from 'Ninanecropolis' (16 November 2008) a Canadian-Iranian who posted, 'You guys are amazing! The first indie rock Iranian band I've heard to date. Thanks soooooo much for making me honoured to be Iranian'. Anita, a young Iranian-American woman said, 'As an Iranian I am so proud of you guys' (7 December 2008).

For young Iranians inside Iran, the band provides a connection to the outside. Some view the band as spokespeople for their generation. On Hypernova's Facebook page Alireza Mi posted, 'I always liked you guys, thank you so much for singing on behalf of us in Iran, Live long, oh blossom of freedom' (3 July 2009, translated by author). Hypernova shows a different side of Iran to non-Iranian audiences, who appreciate and are surprised by their energetic music. One fan compared the group to Joy Division (Fernanda Fernandes, 20 April 2009), but most of the others commented on their own personal relationships with the band or the connection they felt with the music. Hypernova fan Beth Biderman, a musician herself, posted, 'Thank you . . . It is my honour to be your friend. I think your band is VERY special. I also like your tunes, your style, instrumentation, all of it' (18 August 2008).

Geographically speaking, 127 has a wider fan base than Hypernova. This is because they were the first unofficial Iranian rock band to tour outside Iran. In 2006 they performed in Italy and the US and received coverage in print, online and moving image media in Germany, Sweden, Iran, the UK and the US. Many of their fans connected with the band online after seeing them on television. 'SUPER SOCIETY' from Sweden saw an interview with 127 about their socio-political situation on local television and immediately sent them a 'friend request' on Myspace (127, Myspace, 28 July 2008). Pascal (29 November 2008) from France, Tomonari Okada (8 October 2008) from Japan, and Colin Buckley (6 October 2008) from Boston, MA have all posted comments to 127's Myspace page thanking the band for their music. 127, like Hypernova, has a unique ability to appeal to diverse audience groups and to unite them through their music.

From a political standpoint their music provides a great potential for unity in spite of governmental differences. On 127's Mypace page Noam Yatsiv from Israel posted, 'Cool to meet people like you from Iran. If only your leadership was as cool as you, and mine would also be better, I would come see you in Tehran' (12 August 2007). Like Hypernova, 127 also give Iranians living in diaspora something to boast about to their friends. Darius, an Iranian living in the US, said 'Never has anything made me long for Iran as this album [*Khal Punk*] has' (26 September 2008). He added, 'I've added a new purpose in my life and that is helping people find your music'.

Khal Punk, with its new take on popular old Iranian music forms, appeals to Iranian youth outside Iran desperate for contemporary nostalgia in a rock format rather than the pop or classical they've previously had access to through their parent's record collections and the exilic music industry. They perceive 127's new music to be something 'authentic' that reconnects them with the homeland. The very notion of authenticity is highly contested and is something that neither band claims, but it is played on frequently in promotional material for the bands in order to attract non-Iranian audiences craving the exotic. When 127 headlined at the Funhouse in Seattle on 22 June 2008, performing with the band AIIEE!! and Hands of Kali (who were billed as 'Seattle's hottest belly dance theatre troupe' on the poster), they were labelled 'authentic gypsy punk music all the way from Iran!' Thus we come full circle – do bands exoticize themselves or do the media do it for them? These case studies have demonstrated that both are true. The impact these two bands have on the Iranian diaspora, the unofficial rock music scene in Iran, and the non-Iranian audiences who encounter them can be extremely powerful.

Conclusion

Through a description of Hypernova and 127, two second-generation unofficial Iranian rock bands whose aspirations to leave Iran eventually materialized after long battles with bureaucracy, this chapter has further developed some of the ideas about communities and communication, identities and expression that were first presented in the opening pages of this book. As pioneers in Iran's unofficial rock music movement, Hypernova's and 127's stories link back to the beginning of this book, which was concerned with Iran's socio-political and musical history, the middle of the book, which discussed Iran's contemporary unofficial music, and bridges forward to the concluding chapter, which will hypothesize about potential futures for the bands, their generational peers, and their country. The relative success Hypernova and 127 have enjoyed in the US to date has meant that an audience of people outside Iran have been exposed to sounds and images of Iran that contradict those usually broadcast on the evening news. More longitudinal research is needed in order for conclusions to be drawn about whether the bands' sensationalizing of their histories will help or hinder their careers in the long term. Either way, this will be an ongoing aspect relating to unofficial Iranian rock bands, especially as they struggle to gain acceptance in non-Iranian music scenes. The next and final chapter of this book, which is book-ended by quotations selected from transcriptions of focus group interviews with musicians, explores some of the potential futures for Iran's unofficial rock music.

Notes

1 'The great Satan' (Persian: '*sheitan-e bozorg*') is a derogatory term originally used by Ayatollah Khomeini to describe the US; the 'axis of evil' is President Bush's description of Iran, a phrase first proclaimed during his State of the Union Address on 29 January 2002.

2 Iran has one of the highest net emigration rates, according to the CIA World Factbook. A 2009 estimate shows that almost three of every 1,000 people leave the country annually. This figure is calculated by adding the number of immigrants to the number of emigrants and does not distinguish between economic migrants or refugees. Although Iran absorbs a large number of Afghani refugees annually, it has a net immigration rate of -2.62 migrants/1,000 people. See the CIA World Factbook, online resource, https://www.cia.gov/library/publications/the-world-factbook/geos/ir.html

3 Iran's countless conscientious objectors run the risk of punishment, fines and an augmentation to their mandatory conscription time if caught.

4 The rules regarding temporary exit permits are unclear and change often but usually if students can provide a good reason for wanting to leave the country temporarily, for example a conference or event relating to their field of study, they are able to pay a hefty deposit and collect it upon their return.

5 A PDF containing Henley's Global Ranking List of International Visa Restrictions is available from http://www.henleyglobal.com/fileadmin/pdfs/content/HVRI2009_GlobalRanking.pdf

6 *Setar* is a three-stringed Persian instrument from the lute family. '*Seh*' means three and '*tar*' means strings.

7 The most prevalent type of music in Iran's public sphere is street music. Amateur musicians (nearly always men) wander the streets playing accordions, small drums or violins, in the hope that people in the apartment buildings will hear them and throw donations out of their windows. Some street musicians set up at busy intersections and wander from car to car playing folk tunes and collecting money. *Rouhouzi* (lit. 'on the pond') is a comical folk drama that combines rapid verbal humour with colloquial dialogue satirically portraying local people and events (Daniel and Mahdi 2006: 93–4). In late nineteenth-century Iran these dramas would be played out on makeshift wooden stages that were placed over the ponds in the central courtyards of traditional Iranian homes.

8 'No one' and 'Consequences', two songs from Hypernova's EP *Who says you can't rock in Iran?* (2006), are still available at http://www.npr.org/templates/story/story.php?storyId=11182793

9 The discussion threads were started at 'Your Top 3 tracks from
   Khal Punk', from 28 May 2008, http://www.facebook.com/topic.
   php?uid=12803881235&topic=5123 and 'Favorite Hypernova
   Track?', from 28 June 2008 http://www.facebook.com/topic.
   php?uid=7599991543&topic=4888/

10 Halva is a dense, very sweet confectionery that is made with wheat flour and
   butter and flavoured with rose water. It is usually served at funerals and has a
   dark brown colour. Opium, a narcotic sourced from the seedpods of poppies,
   is used recreationally in Islamic societies. It has a pungent aroma that betrays
   its widespread usage. There is no religious decree against the use of the drug,
   which is also a dark brown colour and is eaten or smoked in an elaborate
   ritual. Many conservative and religious people, usually men, smoke the drug.
   It is also prevalent as a recreational drug amongst young people and is very
   cheap due to Iran's proximity to Afghanistan.

11 Khomeini's attempts to stop Iranians celebrating the Persian New Year and
   playing classical music did not succeed, but his actions were not historically
   unfounded. The Shah, when he realized his ousting was swiftly approaching,
   refused to issue public gathering permits for the religious mourning month of
   Muharram.

12 See Baer (2008: 88) and Slavin (2007: 224) for descriptions of Iran's
   involvement with Lebanon's *hezbollah* and the implications of this
   relationship on global politics.

13 An English translation of the Islamic Penal Code of Iran is available for
   download from the Mission for Establishment of Human Rights in Iran's
   website at http://mehr.org/index_islam.htm/

CHAPTER NINE

The 2009 presidential elections and potential futures for unofficial rock music in Iran

Figure 16 Hastily sprayed green graffiti on a retaining wall in a northern suburb of Tehran reads 'Death to Khamenei'. The slogan was tagged over a heart containing the name 'Mousavi', which, although it has been painted out by the authorities, is still visible (photograph by the author)

We don't know even what's going to happen in the next five minutes, so how can we plan for the next five years?
(GIL, INTERVIEW WITH AUTHOR, 1 SEPTEMBER 2006)

Something as simple as choosing tomorrow's outfit becomes a complex state of affairs when the rules and regulations imposed from above are fluid and changeable. In Iran, new laws are often implemented without warning and the public is expected to comply immediately. For example, on the evening of 9 December 2007, at the beginning of Tehran's harshest winter in 50 years, Police Chief General Ahmad Reza Radan declared that women were no longer allowed to wear boots over their pants or winter hats without headscarves (Najibullah 2007). The next day, morals police were arresting women for non-compliance. The quotation above, spoken by poet Gil, was collected on my first research trip to Iran in 2006 and it has proven its relevance repeatedly during the various research phases of this book. Gil's statement became even more pertinent as the 2009 presidential elections drew closer. None of the interviewees wanted to predict the election result, but all hoped for political change.

In focus group interviews we discussed and hypothesized about potential futures for their scene. By presenting their statements I had hoped to highlight the necessity for further research about unofficial rock music and its effect on wider Iranian society. But the events leading up to, surrounding, and following the 2009 presidential elections in Iran have cast even more uncertainty over Iran's future and, in the case of this research, the future of the unofficial rock music scene. Thus, it seemed pertinent to examine the effect that the controversial result of the 2009 presidential election is continuing to have on these musicians.

The first part of this chapter will describe some of the general trends of the Iranian presidential elections since 1979. This description will help to contextualize the 2009 elections but it is by no means comprehensive. The second part of this chapter describes the events leading up to the elections with a particular focus on how the two main candidates, incumbent neo-conservative President Mahmoud Ahmadinejad and his reformist opponent Mir-Hossein Mousavi used global communications technologies to assist their campaigns. Further attention is given to the way that Mousavi's campaign used music to inspire voters.

Music was omnipresent during this tumultuous time, fulfilling its role as a social commentator. It unified voters before the elections, rallied protesters after the final results were announced and lamented the death of the now iconic Neda Agha-Soltan, the young woman whose death was captured by a fellow protester on a mobile phone, published to YouTube and subsequently broadcast by news media across the globe. Iranians inside Iran wrote songs and published them online, Iranians in diaspora used music to connect with Iranians at home and to publicize the unfolding events to non-Iranians in an easily accessible way; and non-Iranian musicians, some famous and some not so famous, expressed solidarity with the reformist and humanist cause through their music. An extended description of the controversial result of the elections is given in the third section of this chapter, which begins with a description of the events as they unfolded on Election Day. In the fourth section I will present a few of the many musical responses to the elections. The book's conclusion, which follows this chapter, will attempt to harmonize all of the ideas discussed in a way that posits a potential coda for the future of Iran.

A brief history of presidential elections in the Islamic Republic of Iran

Historically speaking, the Islamic Republic's presidential elections have tended towards the contentious. This is partly because the Guardian Council, a group of Iran's top religious authorities, vets all of the candidates who apply and they often exercise their power in order to prevent reformist candidates from running. In 2004 the Guardian Council disqualified nearly half of the registered candidates from running in the presidential elections in a move Khatami, the president at that time, labelled 'undemocratic'. Mohammad Ali Abtahi, Khatami's Vice-President, said, 'The situation is like a football match in which the referee sends off one team and invites the other side to score' (in BBC News, 11 January 2004).

President Ahmadinejad's victory in 2005 was also assisted in part by the voting pattern, or rather the non-voting pattern, of reform-minded voters who, according to political scientist Professor Ehteshami, periodically boycott elections in order to protest 'against the reform movement's failure to make good on their promises in the sphere of individual and political freedoms' (Ehteshami and Zweiri 2007: 58). Reform-minded Iranians abstained from voting in the 2005 elections in order to protest against the Guardian Council's vetoing of reformist candidates. Another principal factor contributing to Ahmadinejad's success was that his opponent, billionaire and previous president Ayatollah Ali Akbar Hashemi Rafsanjani (r. 1989–1997), was unpopular with poorer and rural Iranians due to his lavish and flashy lifestyle. Despite Rafsanjani's campaign promises to provide a state benefit to each and every unemployed Iranian, he failed to secure their votes; Ahmadinejad, who had experienced poverty and lived the rural lifestyle in his early childhood was their preferred candidate (ibid. 59–61).

Iran's presidential elections are always intricate affairs. Iyengar and Kinder found that contests for the US presidency are similarly complex because 'they are partly a clash among the major parties, partly an ideological struggle over the policies government should pursue, partly a judgment on the administration's performance over the past four years and a comparative appraisal of what sorts of people the candidates seem to be' (1987: 106). The same can be said of contests for the Iranian presidency, with particular emphasis on the last criterion. Iranian voters are very much influenced by the type of person a candidate seems to be and presidential candidates, aware of this, make their campaigns very personal. Rafsanjani used brightly coloured posters and elitist slogans in his expensive campaign, alienating poorer Iranians and simultaneously failing to encourage reformist voters to boycott their boycott.[1] In contrast, Ahmadinejad's posters were unadorned, he canvassed the country's network of mosques in a small rickety bus and he invited media into his basic home to display his Spartan lifestyle – in doing so he came across as 'a man of the people in touch with their everyday concerns' (Ehteshami and Zweiri 2007: 61).

After Ahmadinejad's victory in 2005, Western governments cited irregularities in the voting process and complained that the election process had been flawed. Their complaints arose from a deep-seated disappointment that a neo-conservative had won, especially after Khatami's reign as president had vastly improved international relations between Iran and the West (ibid. 49–50). While election tampering and vote rigging is impossible to prove, one factor that is not disputed is that institutional support within Iran played a big part in Ahmadinejad's 2005 victory. The Revolutionary Guards and the *Basij*, two conservative authoritarian groups controlled by the Supreme Leader, actively encouraged their constituencies to support Ahmadinejad. During Election Day's Friday prayer session, when campaigning and canvassing in public is banned by law, Ahmadinejad supporters who were in attendance urged members of their congregation to vote for Ahmadinejad and to encourage their friends and families to do the same (ibid. 63). It is not simply the resistance of the conservative clergy and the vetoing of reformist candidates by the Guardian Council that has caused the reform movement to suffer, but the disorganization of the reform movement itself and the tendency of its voters to boycott the elections.

In 2005, the immensely popular President Khatami had no choice but to stand down as he had completed two consecutive terms of four years in office, the maximum allowed by the Iranian Constitution. Historically speaking, Iranian presidents have always served a full two terms since the Iranian Revolution.[2] Statistically speaking, Ahmadinejad was due for his second term in office in 2009. It is also imperative to analyse voter turnout from a statistical standpoint when considering the Iranian presidential elections. The election result has always favoured reformists when voter turnout is high. In 1997, when former culture minister and reformist Khatami was first elected, there was a voter turnout of 79.93 per cent. Although voter turnout had diminished to 66.59 per cent when he was elected for a second term, the total number of votes he received increased by nearly 1.5 million (Szrom 2009). This indicates that it may have been conservatives who boycotted the vote when Khatami was elected for his second term.

After the cultural thaw during Khatami's presidency, the first four years of Ahmadinejad's presidency were characterized by harsh crackdowns and the instigation of the morals police. But from 2005–2009, in the face of an increasingly violent and oppressive regime, Iranians continued to carve out some semblance of social reform for themselves. When Khatami announced he would run for the presidency again in the 2009 elections, anticipation and excitement began to blossom.

Setting the foundations for change: pre-election hype inside and outside Iran

Khatami's previous post as Iran's Minister of Culture informed his policies while he was president and he was very popular among creative Iranian youth. The scores of young people who had abstained from voting in the 2005 elections, after concluding that boycotting had not been as effective as they had hoped, began campaigning through Facebook and other communications media to mobilize their peers into voting for Khatami. Before the 2005 elections they were disillusioned because they perceived that not much had changed while Khatami was in power. But amidst the cultural crackdowns that began shortly after Ahmadinejad's election, they realized that having a reformist president had allowed them far more social and cultural freedoms, however understated these had seemed at the time.

Facebook had been filtered since its inception in Iran, but the ban was lifted in February 2009 as the build-up to the elections began. Ahmadinejad had the ban lifted because he also saw the potential for Facebook to extend his campaign. His plan backfired somewhat as most of Facebook's Iranian contingent comprises young reformist voters. A large Iranian population in exile also uses Facebook to remain connected to their family and friends back home. Khatami was able to use the social networking site far more effectively to generate support. On 17 March 2009, Khatami announced he was withdrawing his bid for the presidency and asked his supporters to focus their attention on supporting lesser-known candidate Mir-Hossein Mousavi instead. Though surprising, Khatami's withdrawal was clever and the transition between support for Khatami and support for Mousavi was smooth due to the parallel usage of global communications technologies by both candidates. For many it was a simple switch between the two on Facebook.

Mousavi campaigners used both classic and contemporary media to recruit supporters when canvassing the country. Posters were pasted to pillars, word of mouth played a large role in generating support and text messages containing information about support rallies bounced from city to city and permeated small towns and villages. An official Mir-Hossein Mousavi fan page was inaugurated on Facebook and had 110,000 supporters at the time of the elections – a majority of them were Iranian.[3] Mousavi's adoption of green as the colour of his campaign was a calculated choice. Green is a symbol of Islam and a colour that resonates on a nationalistic level with Iranians. Mousavi supporters from variegated backgrounds rallied together to get people to vote and to turn green. Facebook and Twitter users made their profile pictures green using Picnik (www.picnik.com) and painters and cartoonists threaded the phrase '*man ray midaham*' (lit. 'I'm voting') into works of art that they saturated with hues of green. The phrase 'I'm voting' was important because its simplicity mobilized young people, who were disillusioned and prone to boycotting elections, to believe that they could effect change.

Mahmoud Ahmadinejad may have plagiarized Obama's campaign slogan when he decreed '*MA MITAVANIM*' (lit. 'we can') but it was the campaign of his opponent Mir Hossein Mousavi that, like Obama's, managed to capture an expansive, disparate and increasingly disillusioned population. Ahmadinejad focused his campaign on coercion, giving gifts to poverty-stricken Iranians suffering under crippling inflation and high unemployment, both of which have been trademark features of his term.[4] Mousavi and his team approached their campaign very differently and notably he was the first Iranian presidential candidate to take his wife on the campaign trail.

Professor Zahra Rahnavard (www.zahrarahnavard.com) appeared alongside her husband Mir-Hossein Mousavi at most rallies and sometimes she even campaigned for their cause alone. Rahnavard may be an unlikely icon, short in stature and demure in appearance, but her background in political science and her role as the political adviser to former president Khatami show the public side of her relationship with Mousavi to be more calculated than coincidental. In one of the most widely distributed pictures of her and her husband, Rahnavard salutes the gathered crowd wearing an acid-washed denim jacket over a jet black chador. Holding a single red rose that matches the floral-printed chiffon headscarf darting out beneath the drab folds of her chador, Rahnavard manages to pull off a mix of chic and piety, appealing to a broad spectrum of Iranian women. Zahra Rahnavard was quick to ascertain an independent identity for herself stating, 'I am not Michelle Obama, I am Zahra Rahnavard'.

Mousavi's main allure was the fact that his policies targeted the Iranian people generally, rather than focusing on the needs of one specific group. The 'common cause' was the uniting feature of Mousavi's campaign.

Figure 17 The remnants of a Mousavi campaign poster, four months after he lost the election, on a stone column near Garmeh, a rural town southeast of Esfehan

The feeling Mousavi's campaign instilled was one of unity, a sentiment craved by many. 127's song '*Baraye fardahaye no*' (lit. 'for a new future'), was written in support of the online cooperative *Setad-e Ma* (lit. 'our campaign').[5] '*Baraye fardahaye no*' describes the diversity of Mousavi's appeal in simple yet poetic language.[6] 127's prose, particularly in the album *Khal Punk*, has tended to be heavily laden with metaphoric and symbolic language. Lyricist Sohrab Mohebbi intentionally used simplistic language in '*Baraye fardahaye no*', arguing that if a song could unite the Iranian people it would have to be easy to sing (Skype interview with author, 13 August 2009). Mohebbi observed that campaigners and protesters were already appropriating either pre-existing protest songs, such as '*Yar-e dabestaniye man*' (lit. 'my old school friend') and '*Sar oomad zemestoon*' (lit. 'winter is over') or were improvising their own words over the rhythmic and rhyming conventions typical of football chants (ibid.).

The lyrics of the second verse of '*Baraye fardahaye no*' are, 'For a healthier state of mind, for better attitudes, for Mr Driver, Teacher, Writer, for the stars on student records, for singers like myself, for this beautiful land, for me, for you, for a new future, go forward' (translated by the author). The 'stars on student records' that Mohebbi sings about was one of Mousavi's most important campaign promises. Mousavi had vowed to annul the star system, which sees politically active university students rated with a corresponding number of stars on their permanent records. Students are 'awarded' one to three stars depending on how subversive they are – a rather euphemistic version of a blacklist and three stars earns expulsion from university and a permanent ban from working in any civil service sector. 127's lyrics also allude to the most fundamental success of Mousavi's campaign – the fact that he united diverse groups of Iranians under one political umbrella. By promising a more stable economy he appealed to the drivers, teachers and writers of Iran and by promising to liberalize social and cultural policies, he also appealed to Iran's many creative young people, including singers like Mohebbi. Most importantly, Mousavi was not going to provide just one future for Iran; he was committed to creating diverse opportunities that would enable Iranians from all walks of life to select from a multiplicity of potential futures.

127's song, which they published to the wall of their own Facebook page, attracted a critical response from one listener, Parham Nik-Eteghad, and a public debate ensued.[7] Nik-Eteghad's criticizm of 127's uplifting song was, 'And this [*"Baraye fardahaye no"*] from the group that sang "It was all smoke (no sign of kebab)" . . . we all thought you understood' (in 127, Facebook, 27 May 2009). Nik-Eteghad is referring in this quotation to '*Hamash dood bood (khabari nabood az kabab)*', the tenth track of *Khal Punk*, which is a song that speaks indirectly about the broken promises of the Islamic Republic of Iran. Nik-Eteghad was voicing the opinion of the many Iranians, particularly those in diaspora, who believe that voting will not make a difference. They believe that any vote, reformist or conservative, supports an inherently flawed, inhumane and undemocratic system. 127's response to Nik-Eteghad's statement was:

> Parham dear, we still believe it's all smoke, but I really don't think that means we shouldn't vote, like those foolish holidaymakers in Los Angeles who argue that we should sit in the corner and wait until it fixes itself (ibid.).
>
> (The 'holidaymakers' 127 refers to are the large numbers of expatriate Iranians living outside Iran who have no intention of returning home.)

Nik-Eteghad's rebutted:

> It appears that those who are going to vote think it will make things better. No sir. This time it will all be smoke as well, there'll be no sign of kebab, and all of that smoke will just blow back into our eyes . . . 'Fool me once, shame on you, fool me twice, shame on me'.

Nik-Eteghad extends the metaphor developed by 127 by saying that the consequences of voting will be dire, that the result of the elections is pre-determined, and that history has repeatedly shown that little can be done to change the outcome. A few hours later Golshan Javadian joined the debate, asking Nik-Eteghad if he lived in Iran during Khatami's presidency. Javadian argued that she would much prefer her friends and family to live under those [Khatami's] conditions than the 'conditions of the last four years' (ibid.). Nik-Eteghad argued back, 'Yes, I was there then. That's my point exactly. Now that they've threatened you with death [Ahmadinejad] you're satisfied with a fever [Mousavi and the reformists]' (127, Facebook, 28 May 2009).

127 responded:

> 'It's impossible to live with idealists . . . We were always in search of the ideal and then in the end we got stuck with this diminutive arsehole [Ahmadinejad]. I'm not happy with a fever, but when I'm living in a place where I have to choose between death [conservative rule] and a fever [reformist rule] I'll choose the fever every time . . . I believe that boycotting those elections was the WORST thing that we have done in these past years and the smoke did indeed blow back into our eyes that time [2005, when the vote was boycotted and Ahmadinejad won]'.

127 were not the only group to write a campaign song for the elections. Mousavi's team supported the recording and release of an upbeat house track featuring Persian rap called '*Mibarim ma*' (lit. 'we will win'), which was produced by Sahand Quazi, who founded *Raplarzeh* (lit. 'rapquake'), Iran's first Hip Hop community, with his friend Shahin Pajoom.[8] His group sang, 'My vote is green, everyone all together, we'll win . . . We sound as one, the enemies are scared, our vote is green and our Iran is proud'.[9] The song, with just over 20,000 views, was not a YouTube success, but it is impossible to tell how far the song spread through Iran on MP3 CD, the format readable by most of Iran's car stereos. Neither their website nor the song they produced for Mousavi's campaign is particularly controversial. Their lyrics do not include the swear words typical of Hip Hop music. The authorities are aware of their existence, but because the group does not put on illegal concerts or encourage illicit behaviour they are not concerned. Surprisingly, one of the traditional folk songs that Mousavi reappropriated for his campaign was the most provocative.

One of Mousavi's campaign videos featured a reworking of the song '*Aftabkaran-e jangal*' (lit. 'those who plant sun in the jungle'), which is more commonly known as '*Sar oomad zemestoon*' (lit. 'winter is over').[10] It is an old communist song, written by the Marxist guerrilla group *Fadaiyan-e Khalgh* to commemorate a battle between its forces and the Shah's powerful army in the thick jungles of the north of Iran. The lyrics are attributed to Saeed Soltanpour, a revolutionary poet who was arrested on his wedding night and killed two months later by the recently inaugurated Islamic government. Blogger Hadi Sedaghat (25 July 2009) argues that the use of the song by Mousavi for his own campaign is unethical because he was a part of the Central Committee of the Islamic Republic Party at the time that Soltanpour was killed. Mousavi was also editor-in-chief of the Islamic Republic newspaper, which was supporting 'both in writing and in political ideology, the violent extermination of the opposition' (ibid.).

Mousavi's campaign video begins with Khatami enunciating his hopes for change as he preaches, 'Sunset is fast approaching, and I love the morning'. This symbolizes Khatami handing over his supporters to Mousavi, who is then represented in the second scene of the video, by a single fist being held high with a green ribbon tied around its wrist. The video ends with Zahra Rahnavard proclaiming, 'I hope that this proud moment will repeat for Junes [election month] and Junes and Junes to come'. This video was watched more than 130,000 times on YouTube. What is most interesting about the use of this song by Mousavi is that it is one of the anthems used by oppositionists to overthrow the Shah in 1979. Other songs and phrases, like *Allah-o Akbar* (lit. 'God is great') for example, which has been shouted from the rooftops in protest since the election's controversial results were announced, were also used to mobilize people against the Shah. Though the same symbols are being used, their significance is different because the context has changed. This relates back to the discussion about Nima's poem '*Ay Adamha*' in the first part of this book. Reworked by Soheil Nafisi, the poem gained new significance in its new context of consumption.

Even though musicians were hopeful that a reformist would win the 2009 elections, that another cultural thaw would ensue and that the Ministry of Culture and Islamic Guidance would once again begin to issue permits for recordings and concerts more freely, there was always a hint of scepticism in their remarks during our conversations. Other scene members reiterated Gil's comment, which opened this chapter. Shahab stated, 'We've got this uncertainty and I think that at the subconscious level this really tortures us . . . My biggest problem is the uncertainty. We don't know what's going to happen in the end' (10 July 2008). Pooya claimed, 'Everything's a dream, everything's fragile. It's possible that in ten years we'll have everything and it's possible that tomorrow we'll lose everything. There's no balance, life in Iran is like this' (12 July 2008). Some musicians were hopeful for their futures, arguing, 'Compared with four years ago it's much better now, and it's going to get better' (Markus, 10 July 2008). They remained hopeful, right up until the time the election result was announced. None of the scene members that I interviewed was predicting the election outcome to favour the conservatives even though, as has been demonstrated in this chapter through an analysis of the statistics surrounding presidential elections, history should have informed them. It was the first time that many of them felt their vote would count for something. They believed it would be a historic election, and they were right . . . but for the wrong reason.

12 June 2009: an election day for the history books

Iran's future was set to change on Friday 12 June 2009. In Tehran and throughout the world Iranians queued for hours to vote. Not even the Iranian authorities had predicted how many people would turn out to cast their votes and many polling booths ran out of ballot papers. There was an 85 per cent voter turnout, the largest since the Iranian Revolution, and the voting deadline was repeatedly extended. One unofficial musician who never usually wakes before midday had already voted by 8.30 a.m. Reform-minded voters were steering clear of mosques and urging others to cast their votes at alternative polling places such as local high schools, concerned that the chance for vote tampering was much higher in those places that were closely connected to the neo-conservative religious authorities. As I watched the events unfold from my home in London on BBC's Persian Television Service in the morning the hype seemed endless. I went with friends in the afternoon to the Iranian Consulate in Kensington to share in their excitement as they cast their votes. Many had never voted before. Before they went in they were excited, but when they returned they were confused. They gathered in groups and discussed what code each had put in the box. They concluded that voting officials inside had given them the wrong code and, because the ballot papers were confusing and the codes for Ahmadinejad and Mousavi similar, they believed that they might inadvertently have voted for Ahmadinejad. Nobody I spoke with that day had ever seen queues at the polling booths in the United Kingdom and on 12 June 2009, the queue stretched around the corner from the consulate until the polling booth closed (see Figure 18).

Just a few hours after voting had closed conflicting election results were already being published, even though counting was manual and it should have taken far longer to tally the votes. Both candidates claimed victory on their websites but, over the course of the next 24 hours, Ayatollah Khamenei declared Ahmadinejad to be the winner, citing a landslide election result. I do not intend to take position on whether or not the elections were fraudulent and thus have avoided a discussion of the main debates concerning this.[11] Whether or not they were fraudulent is not of great importance here. More important is that in the wake of the announcement of Ahmadinejad's re-election hundreds of thousands of Iranians surged into the streets of main cities across Iran in protest. This was the first time since the infamous student riots of 1999 that protests and very violent attempts at suppressing them were captured on film and broadcast globally. Carcasses of firebombed police motorcycles

Figure 18 Iranians queuing outside the Iranian Consulate in Kensington, London, to cast their votes on 12 June 2009 (photograph by author)

and rubbish skips lay abandoned in the streets, university dormitories were ransacked, students physically harmed, and the chants of '*marg bar dictator*' (lit. 'death to the dictator') and '*Allah-o Akbar*' (lit. 'God is great') became deafening.

Riot police wearing studded leather body armour inflicted bodily harm on countless people, including two unofficial musicians who were protesting in the streets. One of them said, 'I was in Vanak Square with a few thousand other protesters. I punched a soldier and three of them cornered me and beat me like hell. I had to use my left hand to protect my face. The whole of my left side is black with bruises and even though I'm dosed up on pain killers it hurts when I type' (online chat, 14 June 2009). The government attempted to shut down all access to communications media in order to stop the organization of protests and to prevent the countless videos that were being captured inconspicuously with mobile phones from flooding the international media. Access to Facebook and Twitter was restricted and the mobile phone networks were shut down. The immediate restriction of communications technologies during the ensuing protests demonstrated that the authorities recognize the power of such technologies to unite people. Footage of the protests surged into the public sphere anyway, as Iranian technophiles, adept at skirting the restrictions, posted them anywhere and anyhow that they could. The footage of the events generated a variety of musical reactions from both Iranian and non-Iranian musicians.

Musical reactions to Iran's election result

The musical reactions to the Iranian election result and ensuing protests can be divided into four categories. There were musical protests recorded by famous Iranian musicians in diaspora, recordings by famous non-Iranian musicians expressing their support for the Iranian cause, responses by non-Iranian, non-famous musicians who were moved by the events, and songs written or performed by Iranian musicians from the unofficial rock music scene either in Iran or in diaspora. Googoosh, the pre-revolutionary Iranian pop star discussed in the second chapter, who now lives and records in diaspora, recorded a song called '*Man hamoon Iranam*' (lit. 'I am that same Iran') and uploaded it to YouTube ten days after the election result was announced. She introduces the song with the following soliloquy, spoken in Persian and translated here by the author:

> Our country is going through sensitive times that will determine our future . . . [this song] is the lament of a mother called 'Iran', and she is singing this lament to those of her children that have left her side and are living far away. Iran has been waiting for them for 30 years.

Googoosh's '*Man hamoon Iranam*' is addressed to her fellow expatriates, many of whom have not returned to Iran since fleeing their country at the time of the 1979 revolution. She employs the emotive and metaphoric language discussed in Chapter Two as she adopts the persona of 'Iran' and narrates, 'You have forgotten me, but I am that same Iran'. Googoosh's message also applies to herself, as she is now an Iranian in diaspora. Googoosh remained in Iran for 21 years after the revolution before fleeing in order to continue her career in music. If Googoosh had remained in Iran she would have been unable to distribute this message, which primarily targets expatriate Iranians but also sifts back to Iran, where many still adore Googoosh and purchase her latest recordings from illegal CD vendors or download them online.

The music video for '*Man hamoon Iranam*' visually emphasizes the metaphors embedded in the lyrics. Googoosh sits in a darkened movie theatre watching the chaos unfolding in Iran's streets with her hands clasped in a prayer formation and tears welling in her eyes. Scenes of her wandering through an empty art gallery, its walls adorned with posters of protesters in the streets, are interspersed with close-ups of her singing the song's emotive verses. These scenes show the disjuncture between Iranians in diaspora and Iranians at home. In the chorus she sings, 'Don't forget me, I know I am ruined, but are you hearing my cries? I am that same Iran'.

The song that received the most views on YouTube featured Armenian-Iranian singer Andy Madadian performing the Lieber and Stoller standard

'Stand by Me' with Jon Bon Jovi, Richie Sambora and a host of other musicians and singers. It had been viewed more than 6,000,000 times as of July 2011. Madadian (b. 1958) is an immensely popular post-revolutionary musician who has released 15 albums in exile.[12] At the beginning of the video Bon Jovi holds up an A3 piece of paper upon which is written 'ma yeki hastim' (lit. 'we are one'). He then sings a loosely translated version of the song's original lyrics in Persian. Andy sings a verse in English before singing the chorus with Bon Jovi. They then switch languages. Iranians are enamoured by foreigners who can speak Persian and although most of the comments posted to the video's page facilitate an argument among some YouTube users about whether Andy is Armenian, Iranian or Persian (he is Armenian-Iranian), many of the other comments illustrate the love Iranians hold for foreigners speaking Persian. Bon Jovi sings in Persian, 'Hand in hand, with one voice, we are compatriots, your pain is my pain, stand by me'.

In addition, Joan Baez reincarnated her 1969 version of the protest song 'We shall overcome' to show her support for the Iranian people. At a concert on the Santa Monica Pier on 9 July 2009 she performed 'We shall overcome', singing the chorus in Persian. It was translated as, '*Ma pirooz mishim ye rooz, az tahe ghalb bar in bavaram, ma pirooz mishim*' (lit. 'one day we will be victorious, I believe this from the bottom of my heart, we will be victorious'). When Baez performed the song again at a free concert in Stern Grove, San Francisco, three days later she dedicated it to the Iranian people. A self-recorded video of Baez singing the song at her home was posted to YouTube on 25 June 2009. This, and the song by Madadian and Bon Jovi, received a plethora of positive reactions. Iranians were overwhelmed by the support that foreign superstars were bestowing upon them. They did wish, however, that the governments of the West would stand up for them too. One friend commented, 'I wish the EU and the USA wouldn't recognize him [Ahmadinejad] as the winner . . . if only one EU country would stand up and do that I guess the rest would do the same' (personal communication via email, 16 June 2009).

YouTube user 'Roothub' posted 'Song for Neda' to his personal channel on 22 June 2009, the same day that Googoosh's song was uploaded. The unknown musician sings, 'Far from the fire and the riots and the violence, I do not feel the same as I did yesterday, now I've seen blood [and] screams of terror on computer screens, Twitters and Flickrs, oh I did not know your name 'til today'. Roothub's lyrics highlight how social networking sites like Twitter, Flickr and Facebook can connect people with distant turmoil. The videos that were uploaded to the internet in the months following Ahmadinejad's controversial re-election were so violently graphic that everyone who came across them felt affected. Roothub's lyrics attest to the fact that no matter how far removed viewers were geographically, the immense power of the bloodshed and terror, mediated as it was through our computer and television monitors, was particularly affecting. It was the first time that footage of large-scale internal anti-government protests from Iran were being distributed across the globe, and these new images were very different from the more usual footage of state-organized anti-American and anti-Zionist street marches.

In some sense, the broadcast of these protests in global news media and on YouTube has opened up a new understanding of Iran's internal politics and the diversity of its peoples. One of the most surprising things for me was the fact that rather than inspire musicians inside Iran to create, the events following the announcement of the election result had the opposite effect. Of all of the musicians that I re-interviewed while I was in Iran in September 2009, only one of them had recorded a track in the wake of the protests and they did not promote it widely. In addition, the atmosphere felt very different from what it was just one year before. From July 2007–2008 there were parties nearly every night at one scene member or another's house. There were impromptu jam sessions, recording sessions, and people were driven to create. When I revisited them in September 2009 those same musicians were doing very little in terms of production. Depression prevailed and many of the musicians were more pre-occupied than usual with planning to leave Iran. A substantial number of them, including Bijan Moosavi, the Yellow Dogs, FONT and the Free Keys have been successful since.

When I began this project I sincerely and perhaps naïvely believed that the future would soon be brighter for unofficial rock music inside Iran's borders. That hope grew as Election Day drew nearer and the support for Mir-Hossein Mousavi seemed infallible. Perhaps we were all naïve or maybe we just needed to hope. When we discussed the future of unofficial rock music in Iran in focus group interviews between July 2007 and July 2008, nobody predicted this outcome as one of the potential futures. Everybody was predicting the situation to get better rather than worse. I will let my friends conclude this chapter with their words. They hoped that by continuing to produce music they would eventually effect change. Shahab said, 'My main goal is to make a difference . . . to say the things I want to say . . . For me it's just about making a difference' (10 July 2008).

> Five years ago, Iranian music was 20 years behind the rest of the world, but now we're starting to hear bands that sound fresh. If it improves in the next five years as much as it has in the last five, we'll actually get ahead of the world! (Arya, email, 15 February 2009)

> Nobody can guess [what the future will be like] but it's certainly going to be better than before. (Obaash, email, 12 March 2009)

When there was no internet . . . the avenues for connecting were closed and it was possible to stop it [music] . . . But it's not possible to stop the wall from falling down now. (Soheil, focus group interview, 7 July 2008)

Art moves on itself, because it's in the minds of people. If they restrict it from above, it just moves on underneath. (Houshang, focus group interview, 9 July 2009)

To be honest I've never thought about doing anything except music, because this is the only thing I want to do. And if I couldn't play music I don't think I'd do anything else. I'd go live on the streets I guess . . . I can't even think about it; I don't have a 'plan B'. (Yusef, focus group interview, 11 July 2008)

Notes

1 Rafsanjani was a staunch supporter of the conservatives during the first period of the Islamic Republic. He has become a reformist over time as have many others. His election in 2007 to the position of Chairman of the Assembly of Experts, the panel that monitors the efficacy of the Supreme Leader and has the power to impeach him, did much to empower the reformist camp in the build up to the 2009 presidential elections.

2 The exception to the rule of the double term presidents is Bani-Sadr, who was elected on January 25, 1980 and was replaced by Rajai on 24 July 1981. Khamenei succeeded Rajai shortly after the latter was assassinated 15 days into his presidency. The assassination has been attributed to the People's Mujahedin of Iran but there are people who believe it was an inside job. See http://www.pbs.org/wgbh/pages/frontline/tehranbureau/2009/08/nabavi-hajjarian-may-be-tried-for-rajai-assassination.html

3 Mousavi's Facebook page is available at http://www.facebook.com/mousavi?ref=ts&__a=1

4 Ahmadinejad's most controversial attempt at generating support during his campaign occurred when he sent a team of campaigners from village to village with sacks of potatoes to donate to the rural poor. There was a bumper crop in 2009 and to sell the potatoes would have damaged the flailing economy further by saturating the market. In the YouTube video 'Dowlat-e sibzamini nemikhaim, nemikhaim' (lit. 'we don't want a potato government'), a large crowd that has gathered in Isfahan to welcome Mousavi on his campaign trail chant protests against Ahmadinejad's controversial tactics. See http://www.youtube.com/watch?v=kkjlB5cXmqM/

5 Setade Ma (lit. 'our campaign') was an online movement run by volunteers that encouraged Iranians to vote rather than to boycott. It was supported by graphic designers, photographers, cartoonists, film-makers and musicians,

who were all invited to donate their work to the cause. See the official website at http://www.setadema.com/index.php

6 A YouTube video called '*Raee midim baraye fardahaye no – 127 va setad-e ma*' (lit. 'we'll vote for a new future – 127 and our campaign') was made 127's election song and is available at http://www.youtube.com/watch?v=iHtqkkwvzVM

7 A quick Google search revealed that Parham Nik-Eteghad is an Iranian expatriate living in Switzerland. Nik-Eteghad attended 'Razi High School', which was a very wealthy pre-revolutionary French-language school associated with the royalists in Tehran before the revolution. His now defunct blog (last entry 16 May 2007) 'Pastime Paradise' is available at http://parhum. blogspot.com/

8 *Raplarzeh* promotes Hip Hop artists and encourages people to join the community. Though not official, the collective is certainly not controversial. They keep a low profile and have published anti-smoking advertisements on the website's front page, even though the founding members can be seen smoking in most of their videos. See http://www.rap-larzeh.blogfa.com/

9 The video for '*Mibarim ma*' is available at http://www.youtube.com/watch?v=3XpuBSqqlBo. The YouTube 'video' is just the audio track overlaid with a photograph of the group members wearing green and superimposed in front of the statue in Azadi ('Freedom') Square in downtown Tehran.

10 The campaign video that uses '*Sar oomad zemestoon*' is available at http://www.youtube.com/watch?v=RCkSCP22t-Q

11 For a comprehensive debate between two bloggers highlighting both sides of the argument, see 'I didn't walk, Iran to democratic reform', http://www.chicagonow.com/blogs/off-the-markley/2009/06/i-didnt-walk-iran-to-democratic-reform.html. Coverage of the two days following election day, as experienced by Robert Worth and Nazila Fathi in Tehran, can be accessed at http://www.nytimes.com/2009/06/15/world/middleeast/15iran.html?_r=1. An archive of media responses to the elections is provided at a blog hosted by the New York Times and maintained by Robert Mackey, see http://thelede.blogs.nytimes.com/2009/06/13/landslide-or-fraud-the-debate-online-over-irans-election-results/.

12 Andy Madadian is also known for his appearance as a wedding singer in the film *House of Sand and Fog* (2003, dir. Vadim Perelman), a film that features an Iranian immigrant couple and a very depressing storyline.

CONCLUSION

By order of the prophet, we ban that boogie sound, degenerate the faithful, with that crazy Casbah sound . . . Sharia don't like it, rockin' the Casbah . . . Fundamentally he can't take it, you know he really hates it!

('ROCK THE CASBAH', COMBAT ROCK, THE CLASH, EPIC RECORDS, 1982)

The word 'conclusion' seems so final. This book has hopefully shared with you the overwhelming sense of uncertainty felt by the young Iranians who take part in this fluid and evolving unofficial rock music scene. How can there be a conclusion to something that is changing so perpetually? If anything, this book will have generated more questions than answers and this 'conclusion' will ask some of those questions and suggest potential areas for future research in the unofficial rock music scene.

This book's primary intent was to 'provide an account of a rapidly evolving and reactionary music scene, as experienced by the researcher through an extended period of participant-observation fieldwork and ongoing research through and with the internet'. Together we examined how unofficial rock musicians use the internet to promote and distribute their music, subverting the Iranian government and the newly established official popular music industry. The private and contested status of unofficial rock music creates its significance. The lyrics quoted above, from the English punk band the Clash, were recorded shortly after the Iranian Revolution, and were inspired by Ayatollah Khomeini's ban on music. The Clash sing, 'fundamentally he can't take it, you know he really hates it'.

Many of the bands that I interviewed stated that the Clash were one of their earlier musical influences. This solidifies a circle of influence that is being amplified by social networking tools and global communications technologies. The Clash were inspired to write a song by the events that created the particular political context that enforced the illegality of the rock music researched for this book. Some of those illegal musicians have drawn on the Clash's music for influence when writing their own music.

Although the Clash recorded their song before many of today's unofficial rock musicians were born, they are linked by a specific context, in this case a political event. Western musicians frequently borrow musical material from other cultures, but one of the main criticisms that Tehran's unofficial rock music receives is that it sounds 'western'. One of the overarching intents of this book was to prove that rock music is a global genre, which becomes significant as it is performed and consumed in local contexts.

Technology, especially the internet, plays a crucial role in how music is produced, distributed and consumed in contemporary times. The introduction of the internet to Iran, by no coincidence at all, corresponded chronologically with the first public appearance of the unofficial rock music scene. As Shahab suggested, '[rock music] was always in Iran . . . Maybe it was in bedrooms for 15, 20 years, but it was always here' (interview with the author, 10 July 2008). The Iranian government's ongoing efforts to restrict media consumption and in particular to restrict access to the internet and satellite television do hinder the scene by preventing it from reaching a broad audience within Iran. Hopefully in the future the Iranian government will allow all forms of music a wider breathing space and the work of unofficial musicians will gain legitimacy and reach a broader spectrum of Iranians inside the country. As the internet continues to permeate, and unless Iran goes ahead with the plan to 'nationalize' the internet, thereby possessing full and total control over online content, this seems likely.

One of the most important discoveries of this book is that scene members, after years of suppression, are so adept at skirting the system that these restrictions do little to hinder the outpouring of Iran's illegal music to interested audiences. Iran's strict censorship laws have isolated Tehran's unofficial rock music scene from its geopolitical context because, aside from word of mouth, it is difficult for these musicians to promote their work within Iran. Despite ongoing efforts to restrict access to these media, scene members continue to use them to subvert their suppressor.

The idea of the temporary autonomous zone, borrowed from Hakim Bey (1990), is most befitting of this scene. A philosophical concept, it applies to every element of the everyday lives of these musicians. Scene members are experts at changing their behaviour to match the requirements of the many different social environments that they inhabit on a daily basis. They must suppress their true selves when appearing in public, going to the grocery store, sitting in a café or attending classes at university. Public social life is full of unknowns, which also contributes to the high rate of paranoia that I witnessed, and at some points experienced, when living in the Islamic Republic of Iran.

After a year of living in Iran I became accustomed to switching between the different persona that my life required. Different social contexts required me to act differently: the researcher, the friend, the student, the foreigner, the musician and sometimes the confidante all spoke and deferred to acquaintances in different ways. Although this may sound like a cliché, when we crossed the threshold into a private space and removed the excess layer of outerwear required by the Islamic Republic there was an immediate change in the atmosphere. We had now entered a zone over which we had temporary autonomy, and the masks could be removed, physically and metaphorically.

The risks of exposing these divergent identities in the public domain are very real; scene members have been arrested for wearing incorrect clothing, having mildly outlandish hairstyles or socializing with non-familial members of the opposite sex in public. Some have been flogged for more serious crimes like drinking alcohol at mixed-gender parties. Because divergent identities cannot be experimented with safely in public, they are experimented with in private spaces and through writing, performing and consuming illegal rock music. As scene members interact with their music (in whatever capacity) they forge their own secret community while simultaneously contributing to global youth culture. When we left the spaces over which we had temporary autonomy, and once again donned our regime-approved outerwear, our transformations were immediate and apparent.

I hope that this book has been successful in presenting a multi-layered description of the continuing evolution of unofficial rock music in Tehran from 2006–2009. The musicians' own thoughts about what their futures might entail were presented in the previous chapter, but this conclusion will end with a summary of my own questions concerning the future of unofficial rock music in Iran. The research methodology for this book brought together a range of traditional approaches, the most important of which is the participant-observer model for location-based fieldwork. What is different about this research, however, is that the 'field' was not limited to one particular geographic location.

Because the internet is central to Tehran's unofficial rock music scene it was logistically possible to conduct much of the research for this book outside Iran's geographical borders. Originally, I had planned to spend three months immersed in the scene in Tehran and to conduct the rest of the research by distance. However, as those three months flew by it became clear that it would take far more time to gain a comprehensive under-standing of the scene. And to do this I needed to experience the every day life of an unofficial musician *as* an unofficial musician. It was only after living in Tehran for six months that I began to feel the weight of the stric-tures of the Islamic Republic of Iran and, after a year, I was very ready to leave.

In the beginning, life in Tehran was a novelty. Waking up in this foreign place, with new sights, smells, people and experiences to encounter every day was, naturally, very exciting. Only after I had truly settled down and the days became routine did I begin to see a more accurate picture of what everyday life in Tehran was like for an unofficial musician. Through the process of becoming an unofficial musician I became privy to the experiences that provided the fundamental data for this multi-sited ethnography. My age and my own interests have very much shaped this particular piece of research, and while my biases are obvious, it would have been impossible to interact with the scene on a personal level for so long had I simply been a 'researcher'. As one of their generational peers I made friends who became interviewees rather than the other way around. Being both a friend and a researcher posed its own set of problems: I felt so enmeshed in the research topic by the end of my interaction with the scene that it was hard to separate myself from it enough to write about it. Parting with this book will be one of the hardest things I have had to do. After analysing the inner workings of the scene for so long during the writing phase, I now feel separate from my friends again. I don't know when, or if, I will ever be able to return to Tehran to visit them.

What happens before June 2013, when Ahmadinejad will reach the conclusion of his second term as Iranian president, will determine the next phase for the future of unofficial rock music in Iran. Musicians will need to push to overcome their geographic and political isolation amidst the inevitable social and cultural crackdowns. As new social networking opportunities arise, how will these be adopted by the unofficial music scene, and will there ever be an increased opportunity for the very necessary face-to-face interaction that the scene is so desperately lacking? With each new generation of unofficial rock musicians the jealousy inherent in the scene seems to dissipate. Once this vanishes entirely, it will provide new opportunities for togetherness and collaboration and when this happens, the stylistic diversity of the scene will further develop and scene members will become more appreciative of each other's work. As institutions like Tehran Beautification Organization attempt to claim back public spaces in order to strengthen communities, the unofficial rock music scene will need to do the same.

New research projects should investigate how the bands that choose to leave Iran fare as they struggle to gain acceptance within the western music industry and how they maintain their ties with Iran through global communications technologies. I am curious to see how many eventually return to Iran, who will be able to return safely, and what will entice them back. I am especially keen to discover who the next generation of unofficial rock bands in Tehran will be. Currently around 65 per cent of university students are female. As they seek out various employment opportunities in diverse sectors and seep into previously strictly patriarchal zones, perhaps they will also permeate the unofficial rock music scene to a greater extent.

The only thing that is certain is that the future of unofficial rock music in Iran is uncertain. I believe that as each new generation of unofficial musicians comes of age, they will, like their predecessors, aspire to effect change through their music. But this research has shown that these slightly naïve aspirations might not be enough to truly effect change and, as more and more musicians leave the country, it begs us to ask how this change will be effected. Can the system be changed from outside Iran? Is a complete overhaul even possible, or does the change need to happen gradually and steadily and from within Iran's borders? In interviews musicians stated that Iran would suffer at the hands of another revolution and argued that the political system needs to be changed step by step, in order for the economy, which is already flailing, to remain intact.

Iranian musicians in diaspora do have the potential to raise awareness of the political and social situation in Iran, but I do not believe that they have the power to effect lasting political change from outside its borders. Through communicating with their audience as they perform and in the ways that they choose to present themselves in interviews with the media, they can open up Tehran's unofficial music scene to the world. But just as pre-revolutionary Iranian pop stars in exile have lost touch with Iran and now portray nostalgic representations of Iran in their music, these musicians will eventually lose touch with home too. It is difficult to foresee the creative industries in Iran opening up further if so many talented young Iranians continue to leave. And the more outspoken they become, the less likely it will become for them to be able to return safely to Iran while the political situation remains the same. While it is difficult to speculate on what might happen in the future, we can only hope that the breaches of human rights will lessen, diversity will increase and Iranians will be able to (one day) be wholly, truly and entirely themselves without fear of repercussions.

BIBLIOGRAPHY

Afkhami, Gholam (2009), *The Life and Times of the Shah*. Berkeley, CA: University of California Press.

Al-e Ahmad, Jalal (1984), *Occidentosis: A Plague from the West*. Berkeley, CA: Mizan Press.

Anderson, Barry (2006), *Persian Perils*. US: Lulu.com.

Ansari, Ali M. (2003), *Modern Iran Since 1921: The Pahlavis and After*. Harlow: Longman.

Anushiravani, Alireza and Kavoos Hassanli (2007), 'Trends in contemporary Persian poetry', in Mehdi Semati, ed., *Media, Culture and Society in Iran: Living with Globalization and the Islamic State*. Abingdon: Routledge, 152–66.

Argheyd, Kamal (1978), *The Role of Value Systems in the Process of Social Change: The Shah-People Revolution of Iran*. Thesis (DBA). Harvard University. Ann Arbor, MI; London: University Microfilms International, 1980.

Arjomand, Said (1988), *The Turban for the Crown: the Islamic Revolution in Iran*. New York; Oxford: Oxford University Press.

—(2000), 'Civil society and the rule of law in the constitutional politics of Iran under Khatami – Iranian president Mohammad Khatami', in *Iran Chamber Society* (online source). Available from http://www.iranchamber.com/government/articles/civil_society_politics_iran_khatami.php

Baer, Robert (2008), *The Devil we Know: Dealing with the New Iranian Superpower*. New York: Crown Publishers.

Baily, John (2004), 'Music censorship in Afghanistan before and after the Taliban', in Marie Korpe (ed.), *Shoot the Singer! Music Censorship Today*. London; New York: Zed Books, 19–28.

Bashiri, Iraj (2000), 'Nima Yushij and new Persian poetry'. Available from http://www.angelfire.com/rnb/bashiri/Poets/Nima.html

Bashiriyeh, Hossein (1984), *The State and Revolution in Iran 1962–1982*. London: Croom Helm.

BBC News (2004), 'New power struggle erupts in Iran'. Available from http://news.bbc.co.uk/1/hi/world/middle_east/3386771.stm

Bennett, Andy (2000), *Popular Music and Youth Culture: Music, Identity and Place*. Basingstoke: Macmillan Press; New York: St Martin's Press.

Bey, Hakim (1990), 'T.A.Z.: the Temporary Autonomous Zone, ontological anarchy, poetic terrorism', in *The Hermetic Library* (online anti-copyright publisher). Available from http://www.hermetic.com/bey/taz_cont.html

Bill, James Alban (1988), *The Eagle and the Lion: the Tragedy of American-Iranian Relations*. London; New Haven: Yale University Press.

Bird, Christiane (2002), *Neither East nor West: One Woman's Journey Through the Islamic Republic of Iran*. New York: Washington Square Press.

Castells, Manuel (1997), *The Power of Identity*. Malden, MA; Oxford: Blackwell.

Chehabi, Houchang E. (1990), *Iranian Politics and Religious Modernism: The Liberation Movement of Iran under the Shah and Khomeini*. Ithaca, NY: Cornell University Press.

Cohen, Sara (1991), *Rock Culture in Liverpool: Popular Music in the Making*. Oxford: Oxford University Press.

Connell, John and Chris Gibson (eds) (2003), *Sound Tracks: Popular Music, Identity and Place*. Oxford; New York: Routledge.

Cronin, Stephanie (2003), *The Making of Modern Iran*. London; New York: RoutledgeCurzon.

—(2004), *Reformers and Revolutionaries in Modern Iran: New Perspectives on the Iranian Left*. London; New York: RoutledgeCurzon.

Cushman, Thomas (1995), *Notes from Underground: Rock Music Counterculture in Russia*. New York: State University of New York Press.

Daniel, Elton and Ali Akhar Mahdi (2006), *Culture and Customs of Iran*. Westport, CT: Greenwood Publishing Group.

DeBano, Wendy S. (2005), 'Enveloping music in gender, nation, and Islam: women's music festivals in post-revolutionary Iran'. *Iranian Studies*, 38(3), 441–62.

Diba, Farhad (1986), *Mohammad Mossadegh: A Political Biography*. London: Croom Helm.

Djamehid, Behnam (1973), *Cultural Policy in Iran*. Paris: UNESCO.

Dreyfuss, Robert (2005), *Devil's Game: How the United States Helped Unleash Fundamentalist Islam*. New York: Metropolitan Books.

Dumper, Michael and Bruce Stanley (eds) (2007), *Cities of the Middle East and North Africa: A Historical Encyclopedia*. Santa Barbara, CA: ABC-CLIO.

During, Jean (1991), *The Art of Persian Music*. Washington, DC: Mage Publishers.

Ehteshami, Anoushiravan and Mahjoob Zweiri (2007), *Iran and the Rise of its Neoconservatives: The Politics of Tehran's Silent Revolution*. London: I. B. Tauris.

Farhat, Hormoz (1990), *The Dastgah Concept in Persian Music*. Cambridge: Cambridge University Press.

Fazeli, Nematallah (2005), *Politics of Culture in Iran: Anthropology, Politics and Society in the Twentieth Century*. New York: Routledge.

Frith, Simon and Andrew Goodwin (1988), *On Record: Rock, Pop, and the Written Word*. New York: Pantheon Books.

Gasiorowski, Mark and Malcolm Byrne (eds) (2004), *Mohammad Mosaddeq and the 1953 Coup in Iran*. Syracuse, NY: Syracuse University Press.

Ghani, Cyrus (2000), *Iran and the Rise of Reza Shah: from Qajar Collapse to Pahlavi Rule*. London: I. B. Tauris.

Ghanoonparvar, Mohammad (1993), *In a Persian Mirror: Images of the West and Westerners in Iranian Fiction*. Austin: University of Texas Press.

Goehr, Lydia (2002), *The Quest for Voice: Music, Politics and the Limits of Philosophy*. Oxford: Oxford University Press.

Gregg, Gary (1991), *Self-representation: Life Narrative Studies in Identity and Ideology*. New York; London: Greenwood.

Greenberg, Yudit, ed. (2008), *Encyclopedia of Love in World Religions*. Santa Barbara, CA: ABC-CLIO.

Gupta, Akhil and James Ferguson (eds) (1997), *Anthropological Locations: Boundaries and Grounds of a Field Science*. Berkeley, CA: University of California Press.

Hadadi, Roxana (2008), 'Concert review – 127 at the Black Cat 7-13-08', in *Blurt*. Available from http://www.blurt-online.com/concert_reviews/view/30/

Henaman, Josh (2008), 'Hypernova – concert review', in *MishMash Magazine*. Available from http://www.mishmashmagazine.com/2008/music/live-reviews/hypernova-12-2-08/

Hiro, Dilip (1987), *Iran under the Ayatollahs*. London; New York: Routledge & Kegan Paul.

Iyengar, Shanto and Donald Kinder (1987), *News that Matters: Television and American Opinion*. Chicago: University of Chicago Press.

Jahanbakhsh, Forough (2001), *Islam, Democracy and Religious Modernism in Iran (1953–2000): From Bazargan to Soroush*. Leiden: Brill.

Javid, Jahanshah (1997), 'The Birdman of Boumehen', in *The Iranian*. Available from http://www.iranian.com/PhotoAlbum/July97/Birdman/index.html

Jebelli, Naeem (2006), 'TAMF: an artistic event or a political campaign?', in *TehranAvenue*. Available from http://tehranavenue.com/article.php?id=533

Johnston, Chris (2002), 'Cool heat in rock lab', in *The Age*. Available from http://www.theage.com.au/articles/2002/10/08/1033538931773.html

Kadivar, Cyrus (2002), 'We are awake: 2,500-year celebrations revisited', in *The Iranian*. Available from http://www.iranian.com/CyrusKadivar/2002/January/2500/

Kahn-Harris, Keith (2003), 'Death metal and the limits of musical expression', in Martin Cloonan and Rebee Garofalo (eds), *Policing Pop*. Philadelphia: Temple University Press, 81–99.

Karimi-Hakkak, Ahmad (1995), *Recasting Persian Poetry: Scenarios of Poetic Modernity in Iran*. Salt Lake City: University of Utah Press.

Kaufman, Gil (2007), 'Meet Iran's Hypernova: a rock band from a country that arrests rock bands', in MTV News. Available from http://www.mtv.com/news/articles/1556532/20070405/hypernova.jhtml

Keddie, Nikki (2003), *Modern Iran: Roots and Results of Revolution*. New Haven, CT: Yale University Press.

Keith, Jeanette (2004), *Rich Man's War, Poor Man's Fight: Race, Class, and Power in the Rural South*. Chapel Hill: University of North Carolina Press.

Keshavarz, Fatemeh (2006), *Recite in the Name of the Red Rose: Poetic Sacred Making in Twentieth-century Iran*. Columbia, SC: University of South Carolina Press.

'King Raam' (2007), 'The art of selling out', in *Zirzamin: the ultimate Iranian underground and alternative music magazine*. Available from http://www.zirzamin.se/?q=node/75

Kinzer, Stephen (2003), *All the Shah's Men: An American Coup and the Roots of Middle East Terror*. New York; Chichester: Wiley.

Kremkau, Bryan (2008), 'Iranian rockers Hypernova opening for Sisters of Mercy', in *ReadJunk*. Available from http://www.readjunk.com/news/music/iranian-rockers-hypernova-opening-for-sisters-of-mercy

Kuruvila, Matthai Chakko (2006), '9/11: Five years later – typecasting Muslims as a race' in *The San Francisco Chronicle*. Available from http://www.sfgate.com/cgi-bin/article.cgi?file=/c/a/2006/09/03/MNG4FKUMR71.DTL

Kurzman, Charles (2004), *The Unthinkable Revolution in Iran*. Cambridge, MA: Harvard University Press.

Lavie, Smadar, Kirin Narayan and Renato Rosaldo (1993), *Creativity/Anthropology*. Ithaca, NY; London: Cornell University Press.

Leaman, Oliver (2004), *Islamic Aesthetics: An Introduction*. Edinburgh: Edinburgh University Press.

Luvaas, Brent (2009), 'Dislocating sounds: the deterritorialization of Indonesian indie pop'. *Cultural Anthropology*, 24(2), 246–79.

Lysloff, René and Leslie Gay (eds) (2003), 'Introduction: ethnomusicology in the twenty-first century', in René Lysloff and Leslie Gay (eds), *Music and Technoculture*. Middletown, CT: Wesleyan University Press, 1–22.

Mahmoody, Betty (1989), *Not Without My Daughter*. London: Corgi.

Marcus, George (1986), 'Contemporary problems of ethnography in the modern world system', in James Clifford and George Marcus (eds), *Writing Culture: the Poetics and Politics of Ethnography*. Berkeley, CA; Los Angeles; London: University of California Press, 165–93.

Mashkouri, Nassir (2009), 'A review of the album *Khal Punk* by the group 127', in *Zirzamin.se*. Available from http://www.zirzamin.se/?q=node/741

McCoy, Alfred (2006), *A Question of Torture: CIA Interrogation, from the Cold War to the War on Terror*. New York: Henry Holt.

Melman, Yossi and Meir Javedanfar (2008), *The Nuclear Sphinx of Tehran*. New York: Basic Books.

Meraji, Shereen (2007), Transcript of 'Hypernova: Illegal indie-rock from Iran', in *NPR (National Public Radio)*. Available from http://www.npr.org/templates/transcript/transcript.php?storyId=11182793

Meyn, Colin (2007), 'Rocking Lolita in Tehran'. In *inthesetimes* (online news source), 18 December 2007. Available from http://www.inthesetimes.com/article/3449/rocking_lolita_in_tehran/ (last accessed 29 May 2009).

Mitchell, Don (2000), *Cultural Geography: A Critical Introduction*. Oxford: Blackwell.

Mitchell, Tony (1992), 'Mixing pop and politics: rock music in Czechoslovakia before and after the Velvet Revolution'. *Popular Music*, 11(2), 187–203.

Moaveni, Azadeh (2006), *Lipstick Jihad: A Memoir of Growing Up Iranian in America and American in Iran*. New York: Public Affairs.

Momtahan, Sima (2005), 'An independent music festival or a commercial competition', in *TehranAvenue*. Available from http://tehranavenue.com/article.php?id=475

Najibullah, Farangis (2007), 'Iran: Wrapping up for winter, and the morality police', in *Radio Free Europe/Radio Liberty*. Available from http://www.rferl.org/content/article/1079262.html

Nasr, Seyyed Vali Reza (2006), *The Shia Revival: How Conflicts within Islam will Shape the Future*. New York: Norton.

Nettl, Bruno (1987), *The Radif of Persian Music: Studies of Structure and Cultural Context*. Champaign, Ill: Elephant & Cat.

—(1992), *Excursions in World Music*. Englewood Cliffs, NJ: Prentice Hall.

Nilan, Pam (2006), 'The reflexive youth culture of devout Muslim youth in Indonesia', in Pam Nilan and Carles Feixa (eds), *Global Youth?: Hybrid Identities, Plural Worlds*. London; New York: Routledge, 91–110.

Nilan, Pam and Carles Feixa (eds) (2006), *Global Youth?: Hybrid Identities, Plural Worlds*. London; New York: Routledge.

Nooshin, Laudan (2005a), 'Subversion and countersubversion: power, control, and meaning in the new Iranian pop music', in Annie Randall, ed., *Music, Power, and Politics*. New York: Routledge, 231–72.

—(2005b), 'Underground, overground: rock music and youth discourses in Iran'. *Iranian Studies*, 38(3), 463–94.

—(2006), '"We have to become universal": internationalist discourses and language choice in contemporary Iranian rock music'. Conference paper at the sixth biennial of Iranian studies, 3–5 August. School of Oriental and African Studies, London.

—(2007), 'The language of rock: Iranian youth, popular music, and national identity', in Mehdi Semati, ed., *Media, Culture and Society in Iran: Living with Globalization and the Islamic State*. Abingdon: Routledge, 69–93.

Ostle, Robin (1991), *Modern Literature in the Near and Middle East, 1850–1970*. London: Routledge.

Otterbeck, Jonas (2004), 'Music as a useless activity: conservative interpretations of music in Islam', in Marie Korpe (ed.), *Shoot the Singer! Music Censorship Today*. London; New York: Zed Books, 11–16.

Paidar, Parvin (1995), *Women and the Political Process in Twentieth-century Iran*. Cambridge: Cambridge University Press.

Pavlenko, Aneta (2005), *Emotions and Multilingualism*. Cambridge: Cambridge University Press.

Petersen, Freya (2007), 'We're from Iran – and we want to party', in the *Telegraph*. Available from http://www.telegraph.co.uk/culture/music/rockandjazzmusic/3664236/Were-from-Iran---and-we-want-to-party.html

—(2009), 'Iranian rockers find their voice', in *Global Post*. Available from http://www.globalpost.com/dispatch/middle-east/090618/hypernova?page=0,0

Pollack, Kenneth (2004), *The Persian Puzzle*. London: Random House.

Poulson, Stephen (2005), *Social Movements in Twentieth-century Iran: Culture, Ideology, and Mobilizing Frameworks*. Lanham, MD: Lexington Books.

Raisdana, Aisan (2009), 'Iranian garage band finds audience in America', in *National Iranian American Council (NIAC)*. Available from http://www.niacouncil.org/site/News2?page=NewsArticle&id=5487&security=1&news_iv_ctrl=1062

Robertson, Bronwen (2005), 'Persian pop music: at "home" in exile and in "exile" at home'. Honours Thesis, Music Special Studies (Undergraduate), Faculty of Music, University of Melbourne. (Abbreviated version published under the same title in *Context: Journal of Music Research*, no. 29/30, 2005: 31–41. Available from http://search.informit.com.au/documentSummary;dn=505530550419389;res=IELHSS ISSN: 1038-4006 [cited 01 Dec 11]).

Rodnitsky, Jerry (2006), 'The decline and rebirth of folk-protest music', in Ian Peddie (ed.), *The Resisting Muse: Popular Music and Social Protest*. Burlington, VT: Ashgate, 17–29.

Rouhani, Farhang (2004), 'Multiple sites of fieldwork: a personal reflection'. *Iranian Studies*, 37(4), 685–93.

Satrapi, Marjane (2006), 'How can one be Persian?', in Lila Azam Zanganeh, ed., *My Sister, Guard Your Veil; My Brother, Guard Your Eyes: Uncensored Iran*. Boston, MA: Beacon Press, 20–3.

Sciolino, Elaine (2001), *Persian Mirrors: the Elusive Face of Iran*. New York: Simon & Schuster.

Sedaghat, Hadi (2009), 'Mousavi uses poem and song by those he killed'. Blog post available from http://truthaboutiran.wordpress.com/2009/07/25/mousavi-uses-poem-and-song-by-those-he-killed/

Sedghi, Hamideh (2007), *Women and Politics in Iran: Veiling, Unveiling, and Reveiling*. Cambridge: Cambridge University Press.

Seliktar, Ofira (2000), *Failing the Crystal Ball Test: The Carter Administration and the Fundamentalist Revolution in Iran*. Westport, CT: Praeger.

Shahabi, Mahmood (2008), 'The Iranian moral panic over video: a brief history and a policy analysis', in Mehdi Semati, ed., *Media, Culture and Society and Iran: Living with Globalization and the Islamic State*. Abingdon: Routledge, 111–29.

Shahidi, Hossein (2007), *Journalism in Iran: from Mission to Profession*. London: Routledge.

Shiloah, Amnon (1995), *Music in the World of Islam: a Socio-Cultural Study*. Aldershot: Scholar Press.

Sidewalk (2005), 'TA Music Festival', in *TehranAvenue.com*. Available online from http://www.tehranavenue.com/article.php?id=463.

Slavin, Barbara (2007), *Bitter Friends, Bosom Enemies: Iran, The US, and the Twisted Path to Confrontation*. New York: St Martin's Press.

Smethurst, James (2006), 'Everyday people: popular music, race and the articulation and formation of class identity in the United States', in Ian Peddie, ed., *The Resisting Muse: Popular Music and Social Protest*. Burlington, VT: Ashgate, 75–88.

Sprout, Harold and Margaret Sprout (1965). *The Ecological Perspective on Human Affairs: with Special Reference to International Politics*. Princeton, NJ: Princeton University Press.

Sublette, Ned (2004), *Cuba and its Music: From the First Drums to the Mambo*. Chicago: Chicago Review Press.

Szrom, Charlie (2009), 'Historical data on Iranian presidential elections', in *IranTracker*. Available from http://www.irantracker.org/analysis/historical-data-iranian-presidential-elections

Tachau, Frank (1994), 'Political Parties of the Middle East and North Africa'. London: Mansell.

Talatoff, Kamran (1997), 'Persian or Farsi? The debate continues'. *The Iranian*. Available from http://www.iranian.com/Features/Dec97/Persian/

Taylor, Timothy (2007), *Beyond Exoticism: Western Music and the World*. Durham, NC; London: Duke University Press.

Thackston, Wheeler (1994), *A Millennium of Classical Persian Poetry: A Guide to the Reading and Understanding of Persian Poetry from the Tenth to the Twentieth Century*. Bethesda, MD: Iranbooks.

Tsuge, Gen'ichi (1991), *Avaz: A Study of the Rhythmic Aspects in Classical Iranian Music*. Ann Arbor, MI: University Microfilms International.

Vatanparast, Shadi (2005), 'Fajr Music Festival, Alireza Assar's concert and

Pezhvak sounds again', in *TehranAvenue.com*. Available from http://www.
tehranavenue.com/print.php?ln=en&id=311

Walt, Vivienne (2000), 'Persian pop vs the revolution', in *Salon*. Available from
http://archive.salon.com/news/feature/2000/02/24/iran_culture/index.html

Youseffzadeh, Ameneh (2004), 'Singing in a theocracy: female musicians in Iran',
in Marie Korpe, ed., *Shoot the Singer! Music Censorship Today*. London; New
York: Zed Books, 129–34.

Zonis, Ella (1973), *Classical Persian Music: An Introduction*. Cambridge, MA:
Harvard University Press.

—(1980), 'Classical Iranian Music', in Elizabeth May and Mantle Hood. *Musics
of Many Cultures*. Berkeley, CA; London: University of California Press,
269–83.

Zorn, Eric (2009), 'A non-capital idea: lower-case the internet', in *Chicago
Tribune*. Available from http://blogs.chicagotribune.com/news_columnists_
ezorn/2009/02/a-noncapital-idea-lowercase-the-internet.html

INDEX

References in bold italics denote a figure

Take It Easy Hospital (band) 78–9
tasnif 17–18
technology
    cost of 55n. 9
    impact of on scene 33, 40, 50, 83,
        90, 146
    significance of 39, 49, 138
Tehran
    description of in song 62–3
    influence on music 82, 83–5
    life in 76, 113, 147–8
    population of 15n. 11
    riots and protests in 59, 137–8, 141
    Urban Beautification Organization
        of 9–11
temporary autonomous zones
    concept of 49, 98, 146–7
    examples of xiii–xiv, 19, 40, 49,
        53, 63, 64–5, 66, 68, 109, *112*
travel, difficulty in getting visas for
        107, 109, 110
travel, international 83, 91, 93, 106–7,
        108, 124n. 4

underground music 42
unofficial rock music scene 24, 76,
        94–5, 108

conceptualisation of xi–xii, 42
development of 1, 17, 60, 72–3,
        80, 86–7
mobilisation of through internet
        47–8, 71–2
problems in 51, 53–4, 61, 63,
        96–8, 100–2
secrecy of 61, 85, 147

Vigen (musician) 22–4

Western involvement in Iran 3, 5
Western music, influence of 33, 68, 80,
        85–6, 96, 109, 145
women musicians xiii, 43–4n. 5, 100,
        148

Yaghmaei, Koroush 26
Yellow Dogs (band) 67–70, 73, 79,
        90–3, 94, 95, 98–100, 141
youth
    global youth culture 76, 82, 87,
        117, 118, 147
    push for social change 11, 12–13
    religion and 115
YouTube 31, 140, 141
Yushij, Nima (poet) 20–1, 27n. 3